The Original New Agent's Guide

Starting & Succeeding in Real Estate

Mark Nash

THOMSON
—✦—
SOUTH-WESTERN

Australia · Canada · Mexico · Singapore · Spain · United Kingdom · United States

"So, I've got my desk & business cards, NOW WHAT?"

THOMSON

—✳— ™

SOUTH-WESTERN

The Original New Agent's Guide
Starting & Succeeding in Real Estate

Mark Nash

VP/Editorial Director:
Jack W. Calhoun

Executive Publisher:
Dave Shaut

Sr. Acquisitions Editor:
Scott Person

Developmental Editor:
Jennifer Warner

Marketing Manager:
Mark Linton

Production Editor:
Colleen A. Farmer

Manufacturing Coordinator:
Charlene Taylor

Design Project Manager:
Rik Moore

Cover Design:
Rik Moore

Cover Illustration:
Susan LeVan, Artville, LLC

Production House:
Electro Publishing

Printer:
Westgroup

For permission to use material from this text or product, contact us by
Tel (800) 730-2214
Fax (800) 730-2215
http://www.thomsonrights.com

For more information contact South-Western, 5191 Natorp Boulevard, Mason, Ohio, 45040.
Or you can visit our Internet site at: http://www.swlearning.com

Dedication

To all the new recruits looking for a career in residential real estate sales, be innovative, listen to your clients, add value to your transactions, have a plan, and work it!

In memory of Emily J. Nash

This publication is designed to provide accurate information regarding the subject matter covered. It is sold with the understanding that the author and publisher are not engaged in rendering legal, accounting, or professional services. If legal advice or other expert legal assistance is required, the services of an attorney should be sought.

Acknowledgments

The journey of a professional life starts with clients. Without clients, one has no business. A thank-you to all of my clients. All of you have helped contribute to my success and have propelled me forward to achieve my business goals, enjoying a stimulating career.

To the students of The Training Institute, L.L.C., of Illinois who kept asking for a new real estate sales agent book. Those repeated requests for an overview of the life of a new real estate sales agent forced me to reflect: What additional information might I have needed to shorten my learning curve as a new real estate sales agent just five years ago?

To all the corporate relocation coordinators whose professionalism was reassuring in what is often a stressful time for clients. The coordinators have helped my business grow and have provided me with a variety of rich experiences helping individuals and families making life changes as they relocate. A big thank-you to all of the referring agents I've come to know based on reputation, phone relationship, and business-to-business networking who send business to me in my market based on reputation, phone relationship, and business-to-business networking. Special thanks to Jaan Henry of Crossroads Real Estate Network for her dedication and pioneering of niche relocation.

To the managing brokers from across the country who stopped by The Training Institute, L.L.C., of Illinois booth at the National Association of REALTORS® Conference and Expo in November 2001. It was great to receive your requests for an updated, informative new agent book from the management side of real estate brokerage.

To my smart, savvy, and generous friend Patti Ross, IBM, Director of North America Marketing Women's Segment. Meeting Patti was to meet a business soul mate. She is always there to offer her realistic business perspective and to share the successes of our lives. To my partner, Steve Berg, thanks for all of your motivation and support in pursuit of business and life goals and for your professional marketing experience, helping make this book a reality.

Thanks to you the reader. I hope you find the answers to your questions in this book.

Preface

Have you been thinking about a career in real estate sales for a couple of years? Most people do before they start their pre-license education. Gathering information about the actual job of a real estate agent on a day-to-day basis has been difficult for those considering the exciting occupation of real estate sales. In 2001, many new agents at The Training Institute, L.L.C., of Illinois asked me to write a book on "what it's all about." It's the book I needed when I started out in 1997, as I flopped around looking for answers to jump-start my sales career. This book will answer basic questions, provide definitions, and help you plan your real estate sales business. It is exciting to have South-Western roll out this updated edition that includes these new features:

- Job description for a real estate agent
- The importance of having an Internet presence
- Professional designations that help market you
- What to do when your managing broker doesn't have the time to train you
- How to build referrals, your bread and butter
- Prospecting options to the "do not call" law
- What to look for in a mentor
- How to work effectively in a licensed industry
- Updates on mold, insurance, and banks in real estate
- Virtual office web sites, the future of real estate
- Salaried agents, the cure for declining brokerage profits

Take a moment and look at the Table of Contents. You will find ten chapters that cover the information needed to make a decision to enter real estate sales or to jump-start your current real estate sales career. This book will answer your questions about residential real estate sales and offer plans for building your real estate practice. In addition, I'll share my stories. Remember, there are no secrets in residential real estate sales — just good communication, professionalism, sales goals, marketing, and business plans!

CONTENTS

Real Estate Agent Job Description

Summary statement

Provide real estate consumers of residential properties with property information, market knowledge, and real property contract administration.

Type of supervision received

Real estate sales agents have their license held by their managing broker, who is responsible for agents' day-to-day professional activities. In addition, new real estate sales agents often have a mentor or coach in their office.

I. Skills, knowledge, and abilities

1. Skill in reading documents written in standard English text, such as brokerage policy and procedures manual, real estate contracts, disclosures, and license laws.
2. Skill in writing grammatically correct routine business correspondence, such as brief transmittal memoranda, internal operating procedures, and performance evaluations.
3. Skill in editing correspondence for correct grammar, spelling, and punctuation.
4. Skill in speaking clearly and distinctly using appropriate vocabulary and grammar.
5. Skill in processing online e-mail requests for property information.
6. Skill in establishing and maintaining filing system for active, pending, and closed transactions.
7. Skill in word processing to prepare business correspondence, property flyers, and marketing pieces.
8. Knowledge of standard business letters and table formatting to prepare materials accurately.

9. Skill in exercising professional and ethical judgment to solve contractual or negotiation issues.
10. Working knowledge of brokerage forms and procedures sufficient to complete transactions.
11. Skill in interacting with the public, other real estate agents, attorneys, mortgage brokers, home inspectors, and property appraisers.
12. Skill in setting priorities that accurately reflect the relative importance of job responsibilities.
13. Skill in establishing and maintaining that cooperative working relationships with managing broker, office administrative personnel, and real estate sales agents.
14. Ability to self-motivate and organize.
15. Ability to drive automobile.

II. Essential Functions and Responsibilities (Duties required for the position to exist. Estimated amount of time is listed for each.)

25% Marketing: Yourself and property listings
10% Word processing/Multiple listing input and research
15% Telephone, e-mail, and fax correspondence with clients, agents, and transaction participants
5% Document preparation/handling/negotiation
5% Continuing education: Professional/sales development and license law requirements
15% Client meetings: Showing current listings to buyers and brokers and public open houses
5% Sales/Office meetings
5% Traveling to listings, property tours, professional conferences, and meetings
5% Transaction meetings: Inspections, appraisals, final walk-throughs, and closings
10% Miscellaneous: One's small business administration

III. Other Duties and Responsibilities (Responsibilities/important duties preformed occasionally or in addition to the essential duties of the position.)

Duties performed in the sale of a property.
- Agent time and marketing expense to receive listing appointment.
- Marketing material expense and time to prepare CMA (Comparative marketing analysis).
- Actual time spent on listing appointment to review CMA.
- Market knowledge to prepare CMA.
- Actual time to meet with seller's to sign listing agreement and related documents.
- Prepare listing for market. Time and cost to prepare property brochures, order yard sign, take property photos, virtual tour, inputting into Multiple Listing Service, and marketing to other agents and public.
- Time to prepare and hold brokers open house(s).
- Time to prepare and hold public open house(s).
- Telephone calls to set appointments.
- Time spent traveling to and from property, showing property for each appointment.
- Call property sellers with showing feedback.
- Receive; return phone calls concerning property from public and agents.
- Write ads, place ads in local/regional newspapers.
- Receive contract and related documents on property, review and present to sellers.
- Present acceptance/counteroffer to sellers
- Counsel property sellers through negotiation.
- Courier contract for changes, final signatures.
- Courier earnest money deposit.
- If condo procure and deliver condo declarations, by-laws, rules and application information.
- Prepare brokerage worksheet for transaction.
- Change property status in multiple listing services.

- Attend property inspection(s).
- Negotiate inspection issues.
- Contact and forward contract to attorneys, escrow agent and mortgage lender.
- Communicate contract status to property seller and buyers agent.
- Place under contract sign rider on for sale yard sign.
- Set up and attend showing appointments for buyers to measure or have contractors, friends, and family to view property.
- Set up and attend mortgage lenders appraiser's visit to property.
- Ongoing assorted phone calls/e-mail to transaction participants.
- Prepare brokerage documents (closing statement, etc.) for closing.
- Set up and attend final walk through before closing.
- Time spent during and to, from closing location.
- Preparing and submitting final closed paperwork to brokerage on property.
- Expense and time for client gift and thank-you.
- For some seller's: arrange for movers, inspection repairs, snow/ yard maintenance, move out cleaning, utility shut off, winterizing of pipes, etc.

Duties performed in the purchase of a property.

- Agent time and marketing expense to receive buyers call or e-mail to meet with them.
- Floor duty in office, weekly, monthly.
- Attend office sales meetings, weekly, monthly.
- Attend company sales/award meetings.
- Attend continuing education and professional development courses.
- Time to prepare buyers packet for meeting.
- Actual time spent meeting in office for first time with prospective buyers.
- Meeting with prospective buyers to meet with mortgage lender.
- Making appointments to preview properties.
- Previewing potential properties for buyers.

- Making appointments to view potential properties with buyers.
- Accompanying buyers looking at potential properties.
- Attending brokers open houses to view new inventories of homes for sale.
- Write contract, disclosures etc. on buyer's prospective property to purchase.
- Deliver and present contract to seller's agent and sellers.
- Negotiate terms of contract to agreement.
- Counsel buyers through negotiation.
- Courier contract to buyers for sign off on changes as agreed upon in negotiation.
- If condo procure and deliver condo declarations, by-laws, rules and application information.
- Prepare brokerage worksheet for transaction.
- Contact and forward contract to attorneys, escrow agent and mortgage lender.
- Attend property inspections.
- Negotiate issues.
- Communicate contract status to buyers, attorneys and escrow agents.
- Accompany buyers on property showings to measure, meet contractors or show property to friends and family.
- Ongoing assorted phone calls/e-mail to transaction participants.
- Prepare required brokerage documents for closing.
- Set up and attend final walk through before closing.
- Attend closing.
- Purchase client thank-you gift and deliver.
- Assist buyers with movers, repairs etc.
- Post closing follow up with buyers.

IV. Knowledge and Skills

- Real estate sale's or broker's license for state in which real estate sales are conducted
- Continuing education requirements for keeping license current

- Professional development classes for professional designations such as GRI (Graduate REALTOR® Institute)
- Technology education
- Sales and small business management education

V. Physical Demands

- Ability to walk up and down multiple flights of stairs.
- Ability to stand for long periods of time at open houses.
- Ability to place, install, and lift for sale signs in and out of vehicle.

VI. Working Conditions and Environment

- Ability to work evenings, weekends and holidays.
- Ability to work days into evenings.
- Ability to work for several months without having a day off.
- Ability to be on call 24/7.

Address for Success

Your First Real Estate Sales Office

Begin the search for your first residential real estate office.

The search for a residential real estate office is the first decision you will make in this exciting time in your life! Maybe you're reading this before you have started the prelicense education requirement for your state. If you just passed your state license test, congratulations! I'm sure it's a hectic time balancing your new profession in real estate sales, possibly your existing employment, your home, your spouse/partner, and possibly children and pets. Stay focused. Keep your eye on the prize of becoming a successful residential real estate sales agent!

Mark's story:

I started my transition into real estate with calls to various prelicense real estate education providers in my area. I was still working full-time in consumer product sales, representing Fortune 500 companies to mass merchandisers, drugstores and grocery stores. I decided to take my prelicense classes at night, two nights a week for five and a half weeks. The license law content was foreign to me, but I studied, memorized, and brushed up on my math to pass the course and the state license test.

Find the right office and build your foundation in real estate sales.

Finding the right office begins with people you already know in the real estate business. Is anyone in your family in the business? Even if he or she is in a different part of the country, it is worth a telephone call or an e-mail to ask a couple of questions and about his or her perspective of the business. Begin to lay the foundation for him or her to send you referral business once your real estate practice is up and running.

Research your list of first real estate sales offices.

You can also gather information and marketing insight into your
potential new real estate company by going on the Internet and
pulling up their web sites. Take a good look at the home page, the
site map, and "about us." Your clients will be doing the same task
on your web site in the near future. Make sure you include an area
in the web site for agent profiles. Remember, clients can't request
you if they don't know you're available. A trip to the public library
is time well spent to check on marketing programs in newspapers
and magazines. Check on any articles relevant to your potential
new brokerage.

Use your database of relationships as a source of real estate sales information.

Are any of your friends, neighbors, business associates, or their
spouses in the business? If so, ask if you can call them. Even if
they are in another part of the country, contact them. If the two
previous methods have not produced agents, call agents you have
personally worked with to purchase, sell, or rent residential real
estate. Call or e-mail out-of-town agents to develop referrals for
your market!

Cold-call the potential real estate sales offices to gather live first impressions.

So none of the ideas above worked, or you still want more ideas to
ensure that you land in the real estate office that is right for you.
Cold-call various real state offices that interest you. Get a feel for
the atmosphere there by saying, "I'm considering a career in real
estate...." Trust yourself. You'll get information from the people
you talk with. Ask to speak to the managing broker, but if he or she
is not in, ask for the floor person (see Glossary, Chapter 9). You
will have an interesting conversation!

Contact your local board of REALTORS® in your office search.

The local board of REALTORS® is also a good place to go for information on different brokerages in your market. Call and ask for someone who does agent training or recruiting, and say you're interested in a career in real estate. Name the offices you're considering, and listen to the feedback. Certain areas of the country also have professional real estate sales recruiters. Some work exclusively for one brokerage; some are independent and find agents for a variety of brokers in the market. Recruiters are a good place to start to get an overview of different offices within the same company and in the market in general. You can also avoid a sales pitch from a managing broker.

Write your own wish list of real estate sales office requirements.

Some additional questions to consider:
- How far do you want the office to be from your home and daily travel routes? You'll find yourself running to the office to pick up or deliver paperwork, checks, and clients.
- How much do you like to drive? Consider the wear and tear on you and your car!
- How do you want to position yourself in the market as a real estate sales person? See Chapter 7 for brokerage profiles. Perceptions are a fact of life, and you may be surprised at how important positioning is to your clients.
- How much pressure to produce sales volume do you want from your managing broker? Think about it. It's also important to be well matched to your first managing broker.
- What is the visibility of the real estate brokerage in the community you're considering?
- What type of market share of sellers / buyers does it have, and what will that mean to your clients?
- Is it important that you work for a brokerage that has a lot of yard signs or the most listings in the Multiple Listing Services?

Or do you want a medium-sized office where there is ample relocation or referral business? A small office where you can shine with little competition might also work for you.

Mark's story:

My sister knew a managing broker. I met with the broker and was recruited to work as an independent contractor, "sales associate," after I passed my state license test. With my 45-day sponsor card, I was off to my new office and my new career in residential real estate sales. At the appointed hour, I showed up in my business best for the meeting with my new managing broker for Day 1 in real estate sales. Full of expectations and excitement for my future in real estate, I filled out the necessary forms. I met the other broker associates, sales agents, and administrative staff in the office. We walked up the aisle between rows of desks until we arrived at mine. My business cards and announcements were ready to be put to use. My new managing broker said to me, "If you have any questions, let me know."

One thought went through my mind at this point: "I have my desk and business cards. Now what?"

It was quite a point of arrival from a history of corporate consumer products that offered ongoing product and sales training to "if you have any questions let me know." Did I have questions! I took the new agent training that was offered by the brokerage and Board of REALTORS®. The feeling of sink or swim and my dream to be a successful real estate sales agent made me realize that I better get organized, creative, and energized — fast!

So I thought "resource," and off to the library I went. Some of the real estate books had words such as *secrets* in their titles. Secrets? I thought this was business. I need business and marketing plans, sales goals, and bottom lines. I was looking for basic information on how a new agent in real estate sales should structure his or her

business and develop a sales and marketing plan. Day-to-day
information on managing this business wasn't about secrets to me.

The sink or swim got me motivated to avoid sinking by avoiding
secrets. Right then I started to lay a long-term foundation in my
real estate business. It has paid off through hard work, relationship
building, creativity, and the adding of value to my clients'
transactions. I learned that going to closings is what real estate is
all about. All of the issues involved with listing, buyer agency,
contract, and closing aren't secrets; they are business!

What is a managing broker?

Managing brokers perform a variety of tasks every day. These
tasks include management of the administrative staff; management
of office equipment (including temperamental technology);
accounting; the overseeing of physical office and building space;
and public relations with other brokerages, the community, and the
Board of REALTORS®. On the sales end, the managing broker has
transaction-based agent issues and liabilities; advertising listings
and agent, recruiting, and sales agents relations; office sales; and
company management meetings. Add in a healthy dose of listing
appointments with agents, office and broker tours of office listings,
and calls at home on Sunday from you — the new agent. A
professional managing broker is never done managing!

What are you looking for in your new managing broker?

You should like lists! You need to start making them every day to
keep you on track for all of the deadlines in real estate sales. You
need to make a list of the managers you have worked for prior to
real estate. Include what you liked about them professionally and
what you disliked about them professionally. Next list the
professional managerial traits you're still looking for in a manager.
Your final list should include the following: team player, ethical,
outgoing, supportive, teacher, sincere, organized, methodical, and

bottom-line and business-plan driven. Think twice before committing to managers that are or appear autocratic, arrogant, self-serving, distant or distracted, messy in appearance and office habits, or late for your interview.

What to expect at the interviews.

You should have live interviews with at least three different managing brokers before you make a decision. Even if you have decided on one, this process will give you exposure to other offices, companies, and mangers before your first day in your new real estate office. After you set up the appointment for your interviews with various managing brokers, you need to get directions and parking instructions. First impressions do count! Be prepared and confident. Also bring two copies of your resume, your business plan outline (later in Chapter 1), and note-taking materials. Dress in appropriate business attire, carry paperwork in a brief or briefcase. I'll say it again, impressions count. Make every effort not to be late for your interviews. If you are, call ahead and inform your potential new managing broker.

Questions you should ask at the managing broker interviews.

You should select the questions that are most important to you in your potential managing broker face-to-face interviews. You can ask more questions in additional face-to-face or phone interviews before making your decision.

- What is the average length of time agents have been with this company/office?
- What is the existing agent mix in your office — full-time versus part-time and low, mid, and high sales volume producers?
- What's your commitment to agents? What is the company's commitment to agents?
- How many new agents do you plan to add to your office in the next business quarter?

- What sales agent training is available within the company?
- Will I have an office? Do you offer a company orientation?
- Will I be an independent contractor or an employee?
- What should I expect to pay up front if I decide to become affiliated with your company?
- Can any of this amount be deducted from my first commission check?
- What does the company provide — business cards, announcements, desk, long-distance telephone and fax, advertisement of my listings — classified and photo, e-mail and Internet access, postage, board and multiple listing service fees/dues?
- How are the ongoing business expenses I generate invoiced / charged back to me — monthly, quarterly, next commission check?
- Do you have an experienced agent with a similar personality to mine, who could mentor me for compensation?
- Do you have a copy of your company's vision and mission statement?
- Does your company have a procedures manual? Is a code of conduct included?
- What are your expectations of me, as a new agent, for sales volume?
- What will my commission split be? How do I gain more of a split?
- If you have floor duty, when am I eligible?
- Do you give sales leads to new agents? Do you request a referral fee for them?
- Does the company charge clients a transaction fee? If so, how much?
- Am I eligible to receive relocation referrals? Do I need to be certified?
- What are the company sales award programs or national awards if a franchise?
- Is there a dress code for sales/broker associates?
- Are there mandatory sales meetings?
- Will I have access to the office after business hours?

- What should my expectations be of the administrative support staff?
- Does the Board of REALTORS® offer health insurance benefits to its members?
- Will all or part of the company be sold in the next year?
- Would you mind if I talked to a couple of agents of *my choice* in your office?

Questions you should be prepared to answer at your managing broker interviews.

You will be excited to meet and talk with your potential new managing broker and find out if he or she is a good fit for you. Your new managing broker will also want to be assured that you will be a good fit for his or her office and that you can bring sales and the resulting revenue to the office and company. You will be asked many questions about your abilities; I have outlined some potential questions below.

- Why does a career in residential real estate sales interest you?
- How do you plan to get clients and their business? (See business plan, Chapter 1. Present outline you brought to interview.)
- Are you outgoing, a people person? Do you have good communication skills? Do you possess the ability to help people define their housing needs?
- Have you been in sales or sales management previously?
- Have you worked for straight commission before?
- How hard are you willing to work to meet your sales goals?
- Are you self-motivated and disciplined? Are you a self-starter?
- What are your first-year sales goals?

Skills you must develop to be successful in real estate sales.

Working with people you don't know is a large part of being a real estate sales agent. In addition to not knowing your clients, you are now involved in a their personal lives and in one of the largest investments they will make. You will be well served to take in and remember the following tips to help you through your first year in real estate.

- Learning when to talk and when to be silent
- Overcoming objections
- Reading body language
- Learning to price your listings correctly so you have credibility with sellers and buyers
- Developing contacts with transaction providers who will help make the transaction smooth for your clients
- Learning time management skills, so you can maximize your sales
- Learning to recognize the time wasters
- Finding cost-effective ways to market your services
- Developing negotiating techniques that can get you from contract to closing
- Developing organizational skills to manage all of the information in real estate sales
- Learning self-defense and personal safety skills
- Developing prioritizing skills
- Developing a balance between maintaining current business and keeping the pipeline open for future business

YOUR NEW REAL ESTATE SALES OFFICE
COMPARISONS
Office 1

Date:

Name:

Managing Broker Name:

Phone:

E-mail:

Rate the following 1 (low) to 5 (high):

___ Is responsive to my needs

___ Is punctual with appointments and returning phone calls

___ Answers my questions completely

___ Dresses professionally and maintains a professional attitude

___ Practices and respects real estate ethics

___ Explains my compensation and commission structure

___ Will help find a compatible mentor for me

___ Explains business-related expenses for which I'm responsible

___ Believes in my real estate sales success potential

___ Will let me speak to agents of my choice in the office

___ Allows agents to work part-time

___ Has an understanding of technology benefits in real estate sales

___ Understands that real estate sales agents are no longer "keepers of information"

___ Understands that real estate sales agents must add value to the consumer of real estate services

Company analysis:

___ Has new agent sales and technology sales training

___ Is committed to new sales agents

___ Has national relocation affiliations

___ Has market presence and name recognition

___ Has a consistent marketing program for listings and agents

___ Believes agents are imperative to the company's success

___ Charges clients a transaction fee

___ Plans to sell part or all of the company in the next year

___ Discusses whether all agents are required to cover desk costs and what that monthly amount is

___ Explains whether commissions get withheld in full or part until desk costs are reached

___ Explains company policy on allowing nonproductive agents to remain aboard

___ Has company vision and mission statements

___ Has company and office procedure manual that includes code of conduct

NOTES:

YOUR NEW REAL ESTATE SALES OFFICE
COMPARISONS
Office 2

Date:

Name:

Managing Broker Name:

Phone:

E-mail:

Rate the following 1 (low) to 5 (high):

____ Is responsive to my needs

____ Is punctual with appointments and returning phone calls

____ Answers my questions completely

____ Dresses professionally and maintains a professional attitude

____ Practices and respects real estate ethics

____ Explains my compensation and commission structure

____ Will help find a compatible mentor for me

____ Explains business-related expenses for which I'm responsible

____ Believes in my real estate sales success potential

____ Will let me speak to agents of my choice in the office

____ Allows agents to work part-time

____ Has an understanding of technology benefits in real estate sales

____ Understands that real estate sales agents are no longer "keepers of information"

___ Understands that real estate sales agents must add value to the consumer of real estate services

Company analysis:

___ Has new agent sales and technology sales training

___ Is committed to new sales agents

___ Has national relocation affiliations

___ Has market presence and name recognition

___ Has a consistent marketing program for listings and agents

___ Believes agents are imperative to the company's success

___ Charges clients a transaction fee

___ Plans to sell part or all of the company in the next year

___ Discusses whether all agents are required to cover desk costs and what that monthly amount is

___ Explains whether commissions get withheld in full or part until desk costs are reached

___ Explains company policy on allowing nonproductive agents to remain aboard

___ Has company vision and mission statements

___ Has company and office procedure manual that includes code of conduct

NOTES:

YOUR NEW REAL ESTATE SALES OFFICE
COMPARISONS
Office 3

Date:

Name:

Managing Broker Name:

Phone:

E-mail:

Rate the following 1 (low) to 5 (high):

___ Is responsive to my needs

___ Is punctual with appointments and returning phone calls

___ Answers my questions completely

___ Dresses professionally and maintains a professional attitude

___ Practices and respects real estate ethics

___ Explains my compensation and commission structure

___ Will help find a compatible mentor for me

___ Explains business-related expenses for which I'm responsible

___ Believes in my real estate sales success potential

___ Will let me speak to agents of my choice in the office

___ Allows agents to work part-time

___ Has an understanding of technology benefits in real estate sales

___ Understands that real estate sales agents are no longer "keepers of information"

___ Understands that real estate sales agents must add value to the consumer of real estate services

Company analysis:

___ Has new agent sales and technology sales training

___ Is committed to new sales agents

___ Has national relocation affiliations

___ Has market presence and name recognition

___ Has a consistent marketing program for listings and agents

___ Believes agents are imperative to the company's success

___ Charges clients a transaction fee

___ Plans to sell part or all of the company in the next year

___ Discusses whether all agents are required to cover desk costs and what that monthly amount is

___ Explains whether commissions get withheld in full or part until desk costs are reached

___ Explains company policy on allowing nonproductive agents to remain aboard

___ Has company vision and mission statements

___ Has company and office procedure manual that includes code of conduct

NOTES:

**Start your first real estate sales business plan using client
profiles.**

After defining and selecting your new real estate office and
managing broker, you should focus on your business plan. All
plans evolve, but writing down and thinking about defining your
business will help keep you focused in the short run. One of the
first items you need to profile is your client. Who is my client? The
easy answer is everyone! But focusing on certain segments, niches,
and spheres will help you answer everyday marketing,
relationship-building, and networking questions to keep you on
track. Make a list of the people you know from all areas of your
life, which could include current coworkers; professional
colleagues; people from your children's world, your spiritual life,
hobbies, and sport interests; your family and relatives, neighbors,
friends, social acquaintances, and service providers; your spouse/
partner; people from your spouse's/partner's world; and members
of nonprofit and for-profit boards and committees.

Take these lists and begin to look for common issues, personalities,
and demographics. Focus on which of these lists make you smile
or feel energized. You will need lots of energy early on, and
working with segments that vitalize you will pay you back tenfold.
You might choose to do some form of marketing to all. You need to
start building long-term *loyal* relationships. Loyalty is the best
foundation for your client base in real estate. Develop them and
keep them; you'll be around a long time.

YOUR SPHERE OF INFLUENCES STUDY

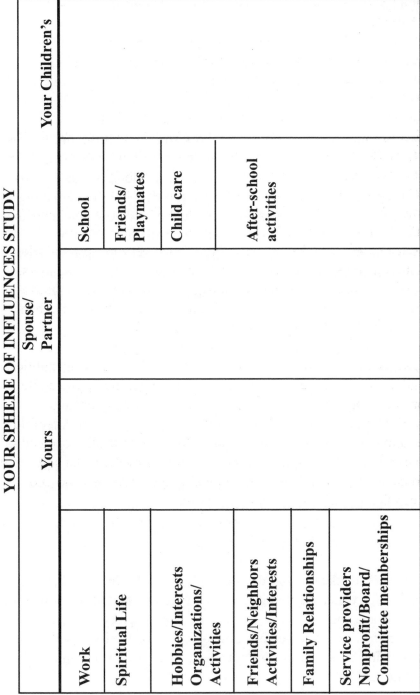

	Yours	Spouse/Partner	Your Children's
Work			
Spiritual Life			School
Hobbies/Interests Organizations/ Activities			Friends/ Playmates
Friends/Neighbors Activities/Interests			Child care
Family Relationships			After-school activities
Service providers Nonprofit/Board/ Committee memberships			

Create your real estate business sales volume goals.

To help you get motivated, establish short-, medium-, and long-term sales volume goals. At this point in your career, you create these goals to measure sales volume through your first five years in residential real estate sales. The rewards should be a reflection of your effort. A good business plan along with effective time management skills will help you work smart. Use the worksheet on the following page to establish your goals for each of your first five years in the business. Each month take a look at Year 1 goals, and see where you are in comparison to your goal. If you see big differences begin to appear between reality and your goal, take the time to have a serious meeting with your mentor, coach, or managing broker to figure out what you need to do to accomplish your goals. If you are happy with where you are, congratulations! Years 2-5 need to reflect the changes you can only discover once you are up and running in the business.

Establish your time commitment to your real estate sales business.

How you reach your goals is a direct result of the amount of time you spend building your real estate sales business. Full-time sales is defined as an average of 50 hours per week. Part-time real estate sales is considered less than 40 hours per week. The days and hours per day are so varied in the real estate business, depending on client needs, that it is difficult to give a number of hours per day. You will also average your hours over the course of the year when slower market times impact lower client demands.

You should take one full day off each week. There is no easy recipe for which day to take. You will see cycles develop with your clients and should be able to take one day off every seven days. Learn how to preserve your time off. Discuss the issue with your managing broker or mentor at the end of your first year in real estate sales.

End-of-First-Year Business Analysis

After your first year in business, you should evaluate what did and didn't work.

Property Listings You Represented in Year 1

Seller Name	Property Address	Market Time	Did It Close Y/N	Reason It Didn't Close	Comments	Sorce of Client *Referral *Relocation	Type of Client *Referral *Relocation *Farm *Open House *Other

End-of-First-Year Business Analysis

After your first year in business, you should evaluate what did and didn't work.

Buyers You Represented in Year 1

Buyer Name	Property Address	Market Time	Did It Close Y/N	Reason It Didn't Close	Comments	Sorce of Client *Referral *Relocation	Type of Client *Referral *Relocation *Farm *Open House *Other

Finding the balance between your personal life and your real estate business.

In the real estate sales business, agents often become reactive from the business. This can be a time management issue, and you should take steps to protect your professional and personal time. Some clients and agents are on call all of the time. You see them with the cell phone permanently attached to their ear! Giving your home number out to everyone is a sure way for your home not to be a refuge from your business. I have a second home telephone number that I give out to clients. When that line rings, I know it's real estate business and can make the decision whether to answer the phone. I don't take real estate business calls after 10 p.m. or before 8 a.m. at home, and my clients value and respect my need for a personal life. You must be protective of your home and personal life, or it will be taken away bit by bit by the business. If you don't want your life to become all real estate, respect your spouse's, partner's, and children's early feedback about your new career in real estate. Success is great when you can share it with someone else!

Transitioning from your current career to real estate sales.

Working full- or part-time in your current career and building your real estate business will take some balancing on your part. In the beginning, let your current employment take priority until you are comfortable with where you're headed in closed sales in real estate. You will see when your priority should shift to real estate. You can't be everything to both careers at the same time, so at very busy points, don't hesistate to refer real estate clients. Referring will better serve your clients and yourself. It will also build a relationship between you and the agent to whom you made the referral, resulting in possible referrals from him or her in the future. You should decide if, when, and to whom at your current employer to announce your new career in real estate.

You've crossed the finish line to your new career and cash flow!

Congratulations! You deserve a big round of applause for accomplishing your goal of making a career in real estate sales. Take a breather every day, and dream about where you want to go in your residential real estate sales career. Now creating cash flow and meeting your real estate business expenses is a priority. As an independent contractor, your compensation arrives when your transaction successfully closes. You can chart your income easily by collecting your transaction files and listing closing dates in chronological order. Is the first one 60 days out, or are all closings clumped together with a few weeks before the next group of closings? Welcome to cash flow! You need to conserve commission compensation when it comes in to pay expenses for business and personal needs. List all fixed monthly business expenses, and add them to your fixed personal expenses. This is the amount you need in compensation from transactions to break even. If you have a particularly successful month, don't splurge until after you have reviewed your cash flow. When is your next successful closing? I preface *closing* with the word *successful* because if the transaction doesn't close or close as scheduled, your cash flow will impact your ability to meet expenses. Save for these cash flow crises!

Salaried agents are an emerging trend.

You might be hearing about salaried agents. In their pursuit to control thinning profit margins, brokerages introduced this type of compensation. The goal is to level out the compensation hills and valleys that independent contractor real estate sales agents experience. It provides brokerage with additional commission income per transaction and gives mid-level producers the expectation of a consistent paycheck, and offers agents benefits. You can inquire at your managing broker interviews whether this option exists.

Commission, compensation, and splits and how they work.

A real estate transaction involves the seller or the buyer compensating the agents. In the traditional model, the listing brokerage pays the cooperating (buyer's) broker a percentage of the contract price or a flat fee. Each agent involved in the transaction then divides his or her side again, equally or unequally, to compensate the brokerage and sales agent. The percentage split with the broker varies according to the agreement. Typically, one keeps more of the split with consistent upward sales volume.

> A property sells and closes for $100,000. The seller pays a commission to his or her listing broker of 5% = $5,000.
>
> The listing broker pays a cooperating commission to the buyer's broker of 2.5% = $2,500.
>
> The listing broker pays a split of 65% of the listing side of the 2.5% to the listing agent:
> 2.5% = $2,500
> $2,500 × .65 = $1,625.
>
> The buyer's broker pays his or her buyer's agent a commission split of 52% of their side:
> 2.5% = $2,500
> $2,500 × .52 = $1,300.
>
> The listing agent receives $1,625 in compensation from the broker. The buyer's agent receives $1,300 in compensation from the broker.

If the system of commission splits is not clear to you, ask your potential new managing broker to explain it at one of your interviews.

Other forms of compensation in the residential real estate sales office.

Productive real estate offices offer other ways for you to be compensated for your assistance. You can learn the business and be compensated regularly by working as an assistant for an experienced high-volume agent. Having your license is a big plus. Seeing how the agent's business runs will give you valuable insight. It's a smart move if you need transitional income, and you'll have a built-in mentor at the same time. You'll know when it's time to focus on your own real estate business.

Some offices need weekend receptionists to answer phones, make appointments, and receive clients before the agents arrive. Typically, these are hourly wage positions and offer traditional paychecks. Ask if your managing broker needs someone to fill in for the regular weekday administrative assistants when they're on leave, on vacation, or ill.

Agents occasionally find themselves overloaded with listing or broker open houses. The time window for these open houses sometimes overlaps, and the agent can't sit. Some agents compensate other agents to sit their broker open houses, especially if no prospecting can be done. Many agents do not compensate public open houses because they believe sitting agents benefit from prospecting potential buyers.

Paying the bills.

The timeline from Day 1 in your new real estate sales office to first successful closing and receipt of your commission will vary. Plan accordingly with your cash flow. The timelines vary with regard to how long this dry cash flow period will last. It depends on when during the yearly market cycle you start, the market in general, your time commitment, your sales training, your self-discipline and ambition.

Budgeting your real estate sales business.

Below are various expenses that may be your responsibility. You should go over these with your new managing broker or mentor to see which apply to you. The flip side of being an independent contractor is paying all taxes and expenses out of your commission checks. Some companies offer programs with automatic deductions for saving a percentage or fixed amount for income taxes and other expenses.

- Professional fees; dues for Multiple Listing Service; and dues for local board of REALTORS®, state Board of REALTORS®, and National Board of REALTORS®
- Professional organization membership expense and travel
- Insurance, errors and omissions, auto (increased coverage), health and homeowner's (increased coverage or umbrella coverage)
- Brokerage mandatory marketing costs, signs and so on
- Postage, courier services, and overnight services
- Stationery, business cards, holiday calendars, and so on
- Auto expense: extra wear and tear, gas, oil, parking, tolls, and loan payments
- Personal marketing program (see Chapter 5)
- Ongoing training in sales and time management, professional designations and technology
- Mentor and coach compensation
- Client gifts
- Referral fees
- Accounting and tax reporting
- Technology, cell phone, pager, handheld organizer, computer, agent sales software, and agent web site.

Choose technology that will give you a return on your investment.

Many technological gadgets are available. You must decide the minimum and the maximum necessary for your real estate sales business. I'm a firm believer that you shouldn't rush out and purchase equipment. Dedicate a percentage of future commissions to invest in this area once you know what you need. Weigh the cost of the development of your own web site and having it seeded in the top 20 search engines versus the client return on a laptop computer or handheld organizer. Choose technology that will give you a return on your investment.

Year 1 Business Plan

Projected Number of Listings:

Actual Number of Listings:

Projected Sales Volume:

Actual Sales Volume:

Projected Gross Closed Commission Income:

Actual Gross Closed Commission Income:

Projected Transaction Sides:

Actual Transaction Sides:

Marketing Plan to Actualize Projections:

Start-up costs:
Professional fees and dues:
Insurance, errors and ommisions:
Stationery, business cards, announcements, and so on:
Desk fees and mandatory company marketing costs:

Actual return on investment expenses:
Listing marketing:
Print marketing:
Direct mail marketing:
Internet marketing:
Agent-to-agent marketing:
Niche marketing:
Business-to-business marketing:
Mentor/coach compensation:

Time management expenses:
Sales training:
Technology:
Professional designations:

Miscellaneous expenses:
Postage, courier, and overnight expenses:
Client gifts:
Referral fees to other brokers:
Auto expenses:
Accounting:
                                          Total:

Chapter 1 Take-Away:

- **Researching and selecting your first real estate sales office**

- **Researching and selecting your new managing broker**

- **Transitioning from your current career to real estate sales**

- **Budgeting your real estate sales business**

NOTES:

Chapter 2

Opening the Door

Getting Started in Your New Real Estate Sales Business

Have you considered having a mentor during your first year in real estate sales?

In addition to this book providing an overview on building your real estate sales business, I suggest that you find an experienced real estate sales agent in your new office to act as a professional mentor. There are many reasons you should consider a mentor in this business. Mentors have the knowledge and can help provide the information you need. A mentor can help you focus on the real issues of your business. Your mentor can provide insight into your local market and the customs in real estate sales.

Mark's story:

One of the biggest mistakes I made early in my real estate sales career was not seeking a mentor. I thought my managing broker would be my mentor — as did the five other new agents in the office! In addition, factor in all of the other responsibilities my managing broker had in the daily management of the entire office. If I had had a mentor early on in my career, I would have been successful earlier on. It's money well spent.

Finding the right real estate sales mentor for you.

Once you have decided to seek a real estate sales mentor, the next step is finding the right one for you in your new real estate office. Ask your managing broker who he or she thinks would be a good match for you. Before moving on any suggestions, take a few weeks to get a feel for the agent dynamics in your new real estate sales office. Observe your potential mentors interacting with other agents in the office and with their clients, both in person and on the phone. You should focus on professional, ethical agents that who have been in the business at least five years and are middle- to upper-sales-volume producers in your market. Your business goals and style should be similar to those of your mentor. Your mentor doesn't have to be your new best friend; your mentor should be a valuable asset in your new real estate sales business.

Compensating your real estate sales mentor.

Think of your real estate sales mentor as a subcontractor in your new real estate sales business. The compensation you give him or her your first year will be invaluable in the long run with regard to your real estate sales business. Historically there has been a high turnover of new real estate sales agents in the business, mainly because of a lack of focused training. Your mentor will be your hands-on day-to-day real estate training instructor for your first year. Your mentor can tell you when you're wasting time with clients who are not going to contract. Your mentor will provide a nudge when you're fixating on processes that are not revenue-generating. Your mentor will give you motivation and feedback. He or she will guide you through successes and failures with clients and other agents.

You and your mentor should work together on your compensation agreement. You may decide that a percentage of your commission be paid in the form of a referral fee. This arrangement allows you to compensate him or her at the same time you have been compensated for the transaction. The exact percentage should depend on the amount of time you are requiring from your mentor. Early on it could be more; then it could decrease as you become more independent in the real estate sales business. You should expect to have a mentor for the first year in real estate sales, depending on your time commitment and sales volume. If you feel the need to extend this mentoring period or to find a coach, do it. The return on this investment will show up in your additional success in real estate sales. Another option is to become a personal assistant for your mentor and receive compensation from him or her while you are learning the business.

When you feel the need to change mentors.

You started out with good intentions and selected a mentor with or without the help of your managing broker. For a variety of reasons, the business relationship did not bring you what you needed. Trust yourself when you realize you need a new mentor. The sooner you find a new one, the sooner you will be on course to being a successful real estate sales agent.

Mark's story:

After my first year in real estate sales, I met an agent who also had had a long-term career in pharmaceutical sales. I was excited about her ability to succeed in real estate sales, as I had come from a similar sales career background.

I inquired whether the agent had a mentor at her new real estate sales office. She did; one had been assigned to her and she was hopeful her mentor could fast track her learning curve in real estate sales. I asked whether her mentor had a similar corporate sales background and a complimentary personality to hers. Not exactly. The mentor had been in real estate sales for many years to add a second income to her family, which was her main focus. The new agaent didn't feel as though they connected at a business level; she was used to a corporate business model and style. I suggested that she see if a new mentor could be assigned to her. She felt frustrated from her first experience and decided she would continue on without a mentor.

Finding the right mentor can be vital to your early success.

Consider a coach in place of or in addition to a mentor.

Many real estate sales professionals today seek the services of independent coaching businesses. These business coaches help keep you focused on your business goals and provide you with business skills that make you more productive. A coach outside the real estate sales office can offer more objective ideas and concepts to use in your real estate sales business. Coaches charge an hourly rate, so compensating them when you use them is the norm. You might also consider a blend of mentor and coach if your mentor doesn't have the time you require but does have the business information and skills you respect.

Learn real estate sales professionalism and business ethics.

The mentor you select must have sound business ethics as well as an easily recognizable set of professional business skills. You must learn to operate this way or you may have financial and legal problems in your real estate sales business at a later date. You should have started your new career with a history of ethical business practices. Think back to your own experience with real estate sales agents. As a consumer, what struck you as ethical or unethical about them? Add the ethical value of what you wanted as a consumer to your transactions as a real estate sales agent. Real estate license laws have become more consumer protection-oriented recently. Once you hold a real estate license, you are in a superior position with regard to knowledge over the consumer in the real estate transaction. State regulators, arbitration boards, and disciplinary committees expect you to follow and uphold city, county, state, and federal laws.

Know it and respect it, federal and state license law.

During your prelicense education, you had to become familiar with local, state, and federal laws relating to real estate and real estate transactions. Most of these laws came about because consumers had concerns during or after their real estate transactions that were not adequately addressed by their real estate sales agents or their brokerages. The laws were legislated to protect the public. As a real estate sales agent, you protect the public by knowing, respecting, and following the law.

The National Association of REALTORS® has mandated that all members complete a minimum of 2 ½ hours of ethics training within every four-year period beginning with the period January 1, 2001, through December 31, 2004.

Know the complaint process.

The public and real estate sales agents and their brokers can file complaints against your real estate license. These complaints can involve single or multiple issues concerning your conduct in the real estate sales business. Complaints should be taken seriously and responded to in the manner and time indicated. The complaint process and response process vary by state and individual Boards of REALTORS®. Become familiar with your local and state process. You should inform your managing broker immediately if you receive a complaint against your license. If there are serious charges in the complaint, you should consider having your own legal representation in addition to your company's representation.

Negative word of mouth by the public is a form of discipline.

As a society, groups of people regulate themselves by talking with one another. At any point, if there are concerns about your business ethics, people will talk. This can do more harm than a complaint to the board. Positive word of mouth builds a business; negative word of mouth destroys a business.

Build your good reputation.

You might be confronted at some point in your real estate sales career with clients or other real estate sales agents requesting you to do something that you believe is unethical. Share the situation in confidence with your managing broker, and determine the best course of action. Do not risk all the time, energy and expense you have put into your new real estate sales business for a short-term gain that can destroy the professional reputation you have worked so hard to attain.

Professionalism is part of marketing your real estate sales business.

Real estate sales professionalism begins with knowledge about the market, the transaction process, and business ethics. Professionalism requires being the voice of reason in what can be an emotional process for clients. The client's first impression begins with the initial phone conversation or e-mail or your introduction at the office or open house. So when you are considering low-cost marketing ideas for your new real estate business, think simple, classic wardrobe and jewelry, clean auto, and organized desk and briefcase. Once you have a client profile as part of your marketing plan, you must get the client to notice you.

Be professional, tasteful, and respectful. You should think seriously about this and know the impact it has on your client's perception of you. How many attorneys, doctors, accountants, and corporate vice presidents do you know who have their personal photo on their business cards? Not many, I would assume, and neither do I. Although some experienced agents would disagree with me, name badges on real estate sales professionals put them in the same realm of consumer perception as the server at the local eating establishment. Business signs on the car and business cards handed out to strangers at the grocery store reinforce real estate agent stereotypes as shown in the film *American Beauty*. You need to stop selling at some point and save your sales energy for existing clients, the ones who will go to closing.

Everyone in the real estate sales profession has cell phones and pagers. When to use them is a professional issue too. When out with clients, you must make them feel as though they are No. 1. Distracting cell phone calls can make them feel like one of your client pack. If I am expecting a call, I am proactive and return calls during a break with clients. Grouping calls is a good professional time management tool.

Be professional in text, voice mail, and faxes.

You must communicate with clients, other real estate sales agents, and transaction support professionals multiple times during the sales process. Learning to communicate efficiently with them will give you extra time to develop new clients. E-mail is an effective form of communication in real estate sales. You can e-mail client listings, photos, and virtual tours; add a note or remarks; and then send. Clients can forward the e-mail and build a consensus on their end about the property before making a live appointment. Keep your e-mail remarks concise and professional until your clients indicate that a more relaxed tone is acceptable to them.

Faxes are used extensively by the real estate sales professional. You will be faxing contracts, listings, and other supporting documentation to clients, lenders, appraisers, title or escrow companies, and so on. Use a general fax cover sheet with information and numbers specific to you and your brokerage.

Business letters are also common in residential real estate sales. They can be letters for prospecting, making agent introductions, thanking clients, and preparing market analyses for third-party companies. Research different business letter formats to determine what style works best for your real estate sales business.

Voice mail and telephone skills are critical to a real estate sales business. Answering the phone and leaving greetings and messages convey an important marketing message to your clients and other real estate sales professionals. Identify yourself and greet the other party in an energetic, professional manner. People will treat you the way you treat them, especially in the virtual world of telephones and e-mail. Return communications as soon as possible.

People appreciate a return call, message, or e-mail by the end of the same business day.

Be aware of privacy issues.

Occasionally agents on both sides of a transaction are from the same real estate office. This situation can be a test of your and your coworkers' level of professionalism and ethics. You should ask your managing broker early on in your new real estate sales career what the policy is on buyer and seller being represented by different real estate sales agents in the same real estate sales office. Be aware of privacy issues that can affect your clients and your transactions with them. Make sure you personally send and receive all faxes during the negotiation and acceptance period. Do not leave documents relating to the transaction lying around. Remember to monitor your phone conversations with clients in case other agents in the office have potential transactions on the same property. Find a conference room to conduct phone conversations and meetings with clients to protect privacy. These rules hold true even if the property is not listed or the buyer is not represented by another agent with your company. You never know when an agent in your office may have a client interested in the same property. The agent may place the property under contract because of what he or she overheard or saw regarding your client's interest in the property.

Be professional when competing in real estate sales.

My first couple of months in the real estate sales business were a real eye opener coming from a corporate business environment. The independent contractor, thinker, and talker versus the top-down, bottom-line, and revenue-driven corporate employee was a big transition for me. I hadn't quite gotten used to all of the schmooze when I realized I didn't have to. My clients were busy, educated consumers and appreciated that I called only with the facts or the answers, not to win a popularity contest. Since I don't believe the real estate sales agent on the other side of the transaction is my new best friend, I don't need to act like we're best friends. Yet I do like to hear their perspective on the market, as the market is always evolving.

Know what to do when your clients believe your competition has been unethical.

If a client notifies you that he or she believes the real estate sales agent on the other side of your shared transaction has acted unethically, ask your client to write down what he or she thought was unethical. Tell your clients that you need to discuss the potential unethical behavior with your managing broker. Bring the client's written document with you to the discussion with your managing broker. Your managing broker can decide what your course of action should be concerning your client and the other real estate sales agent.

Chapter 2 Take-Away:

- **Finding and compensating your real estate sales mentor**

- **Understanding real estate sales agent ethics**

- **Practicing professionalism as a real estate sales agent**

NOTES:

Chapter 3

The Welcome Wagon

Real Estate Sales
Is a People Business

Real estate transactions are a vehicle for personalities to interact.

One of the first skills you need to develop as a new real estate sales agent is the ability to recognize and interact effectively with a variety of personalities. The real estate sale or purchase transaction can have several levels of emotion tied to it. The levels depend on the participants. Some situations (such as marriage, divorce, death, and change in income) may involve individuals who are resistant to change or who want to go full speed ahead. You may experience emotions on only one side of any transaction, but be prepared for the occasional transaction where both sides are emotionally driven. Strong emotions can surface in all personality types at many levels and stages throughout the transaction. I have put the phone down from a challenging conversation where events were moving along smoothly, when suddenly something triggered my client to go off the deep end. To keep yourself from going off the deep end with clients and to keep the transaction moving forward in a professional manner, you need to understand the personality profiles you'll run into with clients.

Mark's story:

A business associate asked me to prepare a market analysis on his property because he and his partner had decided to live together as the next step in their relationship. On a bright spring morning, I arrived prepared to help them move forward with combining their households. The business associate was excited about defining the parameters of his and his partner's new home, which would also define their relationship at a new level. I started with the basic information-gathering questions but was not receiving much feedback from his partner. The more I probed with questions, the quieter the partner became. I realized that something was going on with the reluctant partner concerning their moving in together and decided to focus on the market analysis for the property to be sold. After I finished the presentation, we said our good-byes. The next

day the business associate called to apologize for the uncomfortable situation with his now expartner. Apparently, the seriousness of the meeting to talk about their new home and the sale of the existing home gave the partner cold feet in the relationship, which was terminated shortly after my visit. Talk about real estate being a vehicle for relationships! I learned a lot from this experience. The business associate did sell his home and purchased another with my help!

The experienced buyer or seller.

Let's start with a profile of the perfect client. This person has been through the transaction process before and has researched the other side of the process he or she hasn't experienced. The client is looking for a professional to add value to his or her sale or purchase. Listening to your clients carefully is the key. They are not looking for you to control them or the process; they are looking for you to be a resource to their transaction. They ask informed questions and are looking for honest market-driven answers. If you don't know the answer, admit it and say you need to do your homework before getting back to them. If you mess up with this type of client, your bread-and-butter business will be specializing with difficult clients!

The educated buyer.

Seventy percent of all buyers have looked at properties on the Internet before contacting a real estate sales agent. These are informed and educated clients. These same clients can also access online a variety of information related to their home purchase. Your role with educated clients is to be a resource and a value added to their home purchase transaction.

The first-time buyers or sellers.

First-time buyers are looking for a real estate sales agent to take them through the home purchase process. They need information relevant to their parameters; they also need information about how the transaction process works and about the other participants, from contract to closing. First-time buyers can be labor-intensive for you, but if they are happy with the services and resources you provided, they can be a great source of referral business. Because they were able to do an extensive property search on the Internet before beginning their business relationship with you, they arrive at your office looking for you to add value to their process. First-time sellers have the experience of purchasing, but they still need good marketing and pricing feedback from you in order to place their home under contract. After contract, they need selling-specific advice from contract to closing.

The real estate junkies.

Real estate, for a variety of reasons, breeds stories (some true, some embellished, and some distorted) about transactions, homes, and the participants. You'll find that after people learn you're a real estate sales agent, they like to share the good, the bad, and the ugly about their own, their families', or friends' experiences. I say that I understand, but do not necessarily agree with, what happened and then educate them as to how I practice real estate sales. I might share with them how I would have alleviated the ugly or bad, or I affirm the work of their professional agent. Affirm whenever possible, but recognize that all occupations have some "bad eggs."

The professional residential real estate shopper arrives at every listing appointment ready to speculate on listings price, condition, and so on. They also want to see everything in and out of their price range. You keep showing and they find more to see. They are not going to contract with you. Most likely you could have sold two other properties or prospected for four new clients in the time

you spent with Mr. or Ms. Time Waster. Some people outside of real estate sales like to play armchair real estate sales agent. They advise and question their friends, family, and work associates about their current transactions with you. You need to learn how to react to the invisible source of information your client is receiving. Ask your mentor about invisible sources if they are impacting your transaction.

The reluctant client.

This situation can occur when a spouse or partner decides he or she wants to move. The other half doesn't want to move or needs to be convinced by the motivated spouse or partner. Control issues also come into play in this situation. The spouses might be positioning for control in their relationship through the home purchase. The reluctant spouse might not want to move at all. Don't take sides or get involved in their relationship issues. Figure out early in working with this type of client whether both spouses totally buy in on the new house. Recently widowed and change-resistive personalities might not be ready for a housing change. Family members may be pushing on them. Be patient and allow the client to get up to transitioning speed, or let them know that when they're ready, you're ready. Don't force people to make decisions when they're not ready, or you may find yourself out of this transaction and possible future transactions.

Mark's story:

Several times there were situations with client couples where several dynamics were at work. The main one is when one-half of the couple loves a home and the other person hates it. The next time out they reverse roles; the hater now loves and the lover now hates. Add in some control issues in the relationship, and you have home-purchase gridlock! I offer some gentle counseling each time the love-hate issue rears its head. Sometimes the best thing for these couples to do is sit down independently and list the top 10

features they are looking for in a home. Then they should compare their lists. If they have five or fewer features that match, they need to hold some private conversations before they begin looking for a new home. This process saves your clients from the embarrassment of working out relationship issues in front of you. It saves you time by not continuing to show properties only to find out that it's not the properties, it's the couple's relationship that is problematic in their home search.

The control freaks.

Everyone has dealt with controlling personalities. Most controlling personalities are based in insecurity. I try not to interact with clients of this type. However, I can't avoid them when they are on the other side of a transaction. The best way to deal with them is to keep a professional attitude and stick to the facts. The home sale or purchase transaction involves many people doing specific tasks to get the transaction to closing. Each person has control only over his or her part of the transaction. I let clients know that their reasonable flexibility will lower the stress level in the transaction.

The passive-aggressive clients.

During one conversation they're fine, and in the next they are upset or argumentative. The words *I understand* stated in a sincere manner can soothe your client. Finding out if other issues are contributing to the aggressive behavior can help the two of you move forward. Sometimes you both need a break from the sale process and a new perspective on a new day. Be professional with your clients. Make clear what you will not tolerate in terms of their behavior. By protecting your self-esteem, you will prosper from a healthy one.

Never happy or satisfied clients.

They believe they belong in the next higher price point or want a better location. The problem is their purchase price doesn't warrant either. The problem their expectations. Understand their issues with the market. All clients want the most for their dollar. Say, "Let's make the market work for you." If they continue to fight the market over a long period of time, they may not be ready to purchase. Sometimes I wonder if these kinds of clients think we have secret warehouse hiding their ABC house at X dollars and can place it in their market with a closing date that meets their timeline!

The bankers, attorneys, and trust officers.

As a rule, they view the transaction process as accomplishing a business goal. Future referrals come from successful transactions. Consider marketing to bankers since they have clients who have just moved into your market and opened accounts. Call the trust officer and ask who handles his or her clients' real estate. Follow up calls with letters. Be patient and professional. In time, a listing may be offered to you because, for a variety of reasons, the usual real estate agents are not available. Attorneys are a good source of referrals since they deal in life changes, such as death, divorce, marriage, wills, and so on. Market to them directly or when you meet at a closing or at a title company or recorder office. Introduce yourself and let them know you are available to represent their clients.

Dealing with clients who are more than one of the above types.

You'll run into clients who have one or more of the client personalities just described. What I focus on with clients is to figure out what they want from the real estate market. How do they want me to add to their search, sale, and transaction? If I can satisfy their needs in a reasonable amount of time, with little or no

stress for me and my real estate sales company (and perhaps
receive some referral business), then I continue to work to the
successful closing of their transaction.

Terminating the relationship with unreasonable clients.

The need to terminate a relationship with clients is always a
possiblity in the estate sales business. Occasionally you may find
that your business relationship with clients is not productive for
you or your clients. I have used this statement with clients: "You
might consider a fresh perspective on your home sale or purchase."
This is not the time to place blame. End your business relationship
on a professional note, and move on to other more productive
clients. Watch your success grow with successful clients!

Mark's story:

I had worked with the clients for close to a year. We had looked at
many properties when the love-hate dynamic became obvious. I
stood on the sidelines until they would call and want to go out
again for showings. I didn't believe they would buy. Finally, one
partner convinced the other and a purchase was made. I was asked
to represent these buyers in the sale of their existing residence. I
was hopeful. After placing their existing property on the market,
the hate-oriented spouse called to say the listing price should be
raised considerably! I listened carefully and decided (after many
real estate market education lessons with them) that they should
find new representation. They needed a fresh perspective and they
received one. The new agent got a small price reduction out of
them, the property languished in a strong market, and the clients
had to get bridge financing (a temporary loan on both properties).
The property finally sold at what I predicted early on would be the
selling price. I had cut my losses and moved on to close for several
positive clients in the period I would have been with the armchair
agents!

Client demographics.

Potential clients will come to you from all walks of life. Keeping in mind the previous personality types, let's explore the various relationships you will encounter.

Married or partnered childless couples.

This can be a broad relationship category. The variables are age of clients, length of time the couple has been married or partnered, and where the couple is in the marriage or partnership cycle. Ages of your clients usually represent their level of real estate knowledge. Newlywed couple in their midtwenties will possibly present to you as just married and probably first-time home buyers; they will have developing likes and dislikes, and validation of extended family will be important in their extended home purchase decision. A couple in a new marriage in their early fifties will probably present as having been through real estate sales and the purchase cycle before. They will have established likes and dislikes. The length of time a couple has been together will also impact their decisions. A couple in their late sixties who have been together for 30 years will reach an agreement on buying a retirement home rather easily because they have been through the process many times. A couple in their early thirties who have been together ten years and are buying their first move-up property might have a spouse who deferred to the other spouse on their first property purchase and who now wants a more active role in their move-up purchase. Move-up buyers also look for a move-up property to illustrate outwardly their accomplishments. You will see in your real estate sales business where clients in a declining relationship with their spouse or partner hope that a new house fixes problems in their relationship. I have seen both positive and negative results from this type of relationship repair. You will recognize these clients when the situation presents itself.

Couples with children.

Once in your new real estate sales office, learn as much as you can about the types and locations of schools in your market. School decisions drive most couples with children in their home sale or purchase. You can save yourself time if one of the first questions to your new clients with children is about schools. Be aware of how much your clients want their children involved in the property sale or purchase decision.

Divorcing couples.

A difficult time for everyone involved is when two people decide a relationship is over. The divorce may be amicable or nasty or somewhere in between. You may be asked to represent one or both in a transaction. Maintain a professional attitude with everyone involved, and move the transaction toward closing so your clients can get on with their lives. When children are involved in the divorce and their home will be sold, being particularly considerate to them can help soothe the transition of home and family.

Same-gender couples.

If you don't already know some same-gender couples, you will after being in the real estate sales business. If you are not comfortable working with same-gender couples, find a real estate sales agent who enjoys working with them, and refer the couple to that agent.

Single clients.

Various factors such as age, previous primary relationship, and possible next primary relationship can influence home sale and purchase decisions. The newly widowed or divorced are going through major life transitioning and are quite different from

long-term singles. Some newly singled want this next life period to be short or transitional, while others want it to be forever!

Single clients with children.

Single with children is a significant segment of the population. You might find that the children have a rather large role in the home sale or purchase decision. Information about schools as well as lifestyle issues is important for the single parent.

Multigenerational families.

Families consolidate households for a variety of functional, health, financial, and emotional reasons. The consolidation can be a pleasant or stressful time for everyone involved. Keep in mind that the consolidation will bring together family members who did or did not live together previously.

Dynamics between you and your clients.

A home purchase is the largest single purchase most people make in their life. Clients have many different reasons for what they are looking for from a real estate sales agent. Understand early on what new clients expect your role to be. Don't try to change the business relationship clients expect to have with you, or they might move on to another agent who reads and responds to their expectations.

Do your clients have confidence in the property?

If your clients believe, for any number of reasons, that the property they have selected or have under consideration doesn't work for them, do not pressure them to move forward. Confident clients are a great source of future referrals for you. Clients are not on the same timeline agents are to find and purchase a property they will

call home or have as part of their portfolio. Timing is everything in real estate. Each client is different with regard to building market knowledge, gaining confidence in the market, and making a decision. Patience is a virtue.

Are your clients consensus builders in their new property purchase?

First-time buyers and newly partnered couples often have family members involved in their home purchase decisions. Sometimes these family members are contributing financially to the purchase and are invited or expect to be consulted. Respect these secondary decision makers, and let your clients build consensus in their purchase decision.

Dynamics on the other side of the transaction.

You have worked well with your clients on their search and are thrilled with their decision to purchase. You have written the contract, negotiated the contract, or are under contract on their property. Suddenly a personality on the other side of the transaction becomes difficult. First, try to figure out who is being difficult. It may be the seller/buyer, his or her family members or advisers, the other real estate agent, the attorney, or another transaction participant. Try to address the difficult personality's issue, resolve it, and move on. Your clients will see you in a new light during this important time; be rational, reassuring, resolution-oriented, and professional in your response to the difficulty. Your clients are looking to you for these skills, which they may lack because of their emotional involvement in the property. (See real estate agent types in Chapter 7.)

Dynamics with referring agents.

I always say life would be boring if we were all the same. When another agent refers business to you, be your professional self and factor in different approaches by different agents to the business. Don't allow referring agents to micromanage their referral to you. This is especially true when another agent has referred a family member. Referrals are generally a positive affirmation of you as a professional, but be aware of the occasional geographically removed micromanaging referral agent. Call or send a thank-you to the referring agent after closing a referral client. Create a marketing piece to reinforce to referring agents that you are looking to build your referral business.

The baggage everyone has.

Agents interact with many personalities in everyday life. When the occasional personality match doesn't work out between you and a client, move on. When you run into numerous personalities that haven't worked, you might consider yourself as the reason these matches did not work. You must be a people person to succeed in real estate sales. Talk to your mentor if you have consistent problems meshing with clients, and see what you can do to move forward in the business. These are my beliefs with regard to the real estate sales business: Every one will not like me, some clients have motivations I am not aware of, and I win most and lose a couple every year.

Chapter 3 Take-Away:

- **Understanding real estate transactions are a vehicle for personalities to interact**

- **Realizing that transaction participants arrive at contract with differing viewpoints**

- **Understanding client dynamics and how they impact your role. If we were all the same, life sure would be boring**

NOTES:

Chapter 4

Time Is Money

Training, Time Management, and Professional Designations

How much additional training do you need?

Training is a good ongoing tool for you to use in your real estate sales business. Trying to balance the need for income and the loss of sales time to receive more training is difficult. Several factors will influence your need for more training. Your sales, prospecting, marketing, or technology skills may be weak areas that you need to work on. The ongoing question at this point in your new business is how much income you will receive from this additional training? Will it be time management based, or will it help you develop clients and work effectively to move them to closing? You already have been through training to receive your real estate sales license. Your company as well as your local Board of REALTORS® may have required training. Do you need compensation from a closing before you can give up the time for more training? Are you ready to get into the business of real estate sales after all of the required training and need a vacation from education? Only you can answer these questions. One thing I can share with you is that you will always be in training or education for your real estate sales business.

Mark's story:

You're probably wondering why you must spend more time and money on training after going through the prelicense education. You don't need additional training immediately upon embarking on your new real estate sales business, but in your first year, you will need to receive additional relocation, sales, technology, and other related training. You're never done learning in real estate or in life, especially with the changes in technology, and the real estate business and the required continuing education and ethics courses. Get used to it and enjoy the break from your practice and the opportunity to network with other real estate sales agents. I began additional training during my first year in real estate to learn the relocation business. I found it to be a good mirror of my previous corporate background, and it generated much-needed real estate income. The relocation clients added a new perspective to my life, and I learned so much from clients educating me about various markets, cultures, and lifestyles.

Basic technology skills you will need.

Technology is driving more of the daily routine of productive real estate sales agents. Knowing how to use a digital camera and how to download and view a virtual property tour is becoming the norm in the real estate sales business. You should be able to format and receive e-mail, which includes attaching multiple listing information to send to clients. A variety of word processing and computer marketing program skills are important. Time-effective handheld organizer and laptop skills are necessary if you plan to use them effectively in your real estate sales business. Running a fax and photocopy machine and using a cell phone and pager are everyday skills you will need.

Renewal of real estate licensure, ethics, and broker education.

Your state real estate license has education renewal requirements. These requirements include that you complete some form of continuing education curriculum required by your state real estate regulating authority before the next renewal of your license. In some states, real estate agents who held real estate licenses before the introduction of legislated continuing education are exempt from continuing education requirements. You can also take additional education to receive the next level of real estate licensure in your state. The National Association of REALTORS® also has requirements for ethics training every four years for all members of its association.

Professional designation education.

When you receive experienced real estate sales agents' business cards, some have initials after the name. These initials stand for a variety of professional designations for which the agents have been certified upon completion of educational courses.

Accredit Buyers Representative (ABR): Is a designation from the Real Estate Agent Council that trains experienced real estate sales agents in specifically representing the real estate consumer.

Accredited Land Consultant (ALC): Are the recognized experts in land brokerage transactions of five specialized types: farms and ranches, undeveloped tracts of land, transitional and development land, subdivision and wholesaling of lots and site selection, and assemblage of land parcels.

Accredited Residential Manager (ARM): Is a designation for individuals who manage rental apartment Complexes, rental mobile homes, rental condominiums, rental single-family homes, single-room occupancy apartments, and homeowners associations and for individuals who are resident managers, property managers, or asset managers.

Certified Residential Specialist (CRS): Designates sales achievement in education and sales experience. All real estate sales agents who want to keep abreast of the latest sales and marketing techniques, enhance their professionalism, and increase their earning power can become certified after completing the required course.

E-PRO: Is a training program presented entirely online to certify real estate agents and brokers as Internet Professionals.

Graduate REALTOR® Institute (GRI): Is a designation earned by the licensed real estate sales agent by completing a national program of specialized and advanced education. The program consists of study of special aspects of real estate such as residential marketing, cost basis, appreciation methods, investment real estate, construction, real estate tax concepts, exchanges, capital gains, and various types of mortgage programs.

Recreation and Resort Specialist (RRS): Is available to experienced real estate sales agents who offer proof of successful closed transactions and who complete a two-day core course that focuses on recreation and resort properties.

Seniors Real Estate Specialist (SRES): Is available to real estate sales agents to help seniors make wise decisions about selling the family home, buying rental property, or managing the capital gains and tax implications of owning real estate.

Sales training.

Once you are up and running in your new real estate sales business, you will be offered opportunities to gain additional training in different types of sales and business management. You or your mentor will be aware of the areas you should focus on with additional sales training. You need to weigh the long-term benefits of taking time away from your new real estate sales business (and the loss of potential compensation from transactions) against the short-or long-term benefits of the training opportunities.

Training and education: time versus money.

As a new real estate sales agent, you should have a discussion with your managing broker and your mentor about the financial benefits of professional designations and sales training and how they fit into your real estate business plan in Year 1. After your first year, you will have an understanding of the sales and professional designation needs you should include in future business plans.

Mark's story:

I, like most new agents, didn't have a lot of extra money when I first began my real estate sales business. But after reading several books on starting a new small business, I realized I had to spend money to make money. I dedicated escalating portions of my income for training, marketing, and so on, to help grow my business. I was conservative at first, and each new success pushed me on to greater confidence the next time a larger financial outlay was needed. Almost all of my financial risk taking paid off!

Time management at your real estate sales office.

Time is money. How agents manage the time they have is the difference between the successful 20 percent of real estate sales agents and the other 80 percent. After you have settled into your new real estate sales office, you will begin to understand the office and agent dynamics. Some agents go to their office to enjoy a social experience with other agents or to escape from their home environment. Your real estate office business-driven real estate sales agents go to the office to work their business plans and to keep their real estate sales transaction pipeline alive and well.

The design of your new real estate office can impact your ability to operate at maximum efficiency. Consider how your office is laid out. Is it a sea of desks, with multiple phone conversations bouncing off the walls? Do dividers create privacy and to control noise? Are any individual offices or conference rooms available for you to use when putting together business-related plans or projects or when meeting with clients?

To keep yourself focused in your new real estate sales office and business, you must tune out the distractions and interact with and be aware of the experienced agents at a professional level to absorb their real estate sales skills. Your mentor or managing broker should be the main person to whom you present client or transaction questions. This book is a good resource when you don't want to waste other agents' time by asking them for basic information that is relevant to most real estate sales offices. If you find you are not getting as much accomplished at your real estate sales as you need to, consider a trial period where you split time between the real estate sales office and a home office. Working from a home office requires self-discipline. You should find a space to dedicate to your real estate sales business. The space should be quiet so you are able to speak on the phone and work on all of the details of your real estate sales business. If the trial period at home is positive, you should consider a second phone line, a fax, and other technology equipment to maximize your efficiency.

Is your business time slipping away?

Time management, once you monitor what is revenue-producing and what is the point of diminishing returns with clients and other agents, will set you on track in your real estate sales business. Maintaining communication with other agents in transactions can be a real time saver. It's easy to get sidetracked on issues that are not moving your common transaction to closing. It is more difficult to manage talkative or insecure clients, but your mentor or managing broker should be able to offer you effective tools for managing this type of client. You may, on occasion, need to terminate clients that are not proving to be time-efficient in your real estate sales business. The first time you end a business relationship with clients who have not provided any compensation is difficult. I always look at the up side of terminating clients by the renewed energy and focus I have on other clients. Try "you might consider a fresh perspective from another real estate agent in handling your home purchase or sale." Be professional with clients if you do decide to terminate your relationship with them.

Market cycles and patience.

Market cycles have an impact on your real estate sales business. The first type of market cycle you will experience is the yearly cycle of seasonal markets. Depending on when in the year you enter real estate and where you are located in the country, you might be at the top or low market for the year. In my market, spring market is high; the period from Thanksgiving to the New Year is low. In a best-case scenario, you want to prepare to enter the real estate sales business in the low market to take advantage of the high market.

After seasonal markets, the overall market in general can impact your real estate sales business. Is your market a seller's, buyer's, balanced, evolving market? Discuss with your mentor the definition of these markets in your real estate sales market. High interest rates have a dramatic impact on markets, and creative financing strategies can be effective in high interest rate-driven markets.

Chapter 4 Take-Away:

- **Understanding the alphabet soup of professional designations**
- **Continuing education required by your state to keep your license compliant**
- **Researching technology and what benefits that it brings to you and your clients**
- **Accepting the need for ongoing sales, marketing, and time management training**

NOTES:

Chapter 5

Spread It Around the Neighborhood

The Real Estate Business Revolves Around Marketing

Understanding consumer products marketing.

When consumers go to your local real estate market to purchase or sell a home, the home is the product they are buying or selling. The bundle of real estate services in the transaction process is what you sell to the consumer. The consumer is motivated to enter the market by the end product, or the home. An agent's services are the consumer's perceived value of what the real estate sales agent adds to the product purchase. You should keep this consumer perspective in mind throughout your real estate sales career. Without the consumer being driven by the need to buy or sell property, agents have no basis for their business. The consumer can choose from a variety of service providers or real estate sales agents. Adding value to the transaction for clients is the goal. This will define and build a real estate sales business.

Marketing your business skills versus listing-based marketing.

Historically in real estate marketing, real estate sales agents focus most of their marketing dollars on advertising their listings to the public. When I started in the real estate sales business, I wanted to follow some recent consumer product marketing strategies. In addition to marketing my listings, I wanted to start branding my real estate sales practices. These practices included offering consumers as much information as I had about the transaction process and the market—and not be the keeper of the information. I realized consumers had access to as much market inventory and sales information as I did, so I needed to find new benefits and values to add to their process. Niche or target (speciality or interest-based consumer groups) marketing allowed me to focus and build relationships first and to market my real estate transactions services second. Building relationships first and marketing myself later was contrary to established practices in real estate sales. Most agents want to prospect today, show property tomorrow, and write transactions on the weekend. I wanted a more loyal relationship-based real estate sales business based on the value I brought to my clients' transactions.

Preselling through relationship building.

When my phone rings at the real estate sales office, the call is typically from a client referral, a business relationship referral, or an agent referral. The phone ringing today is the result of many months and years of laying my relationship-based real estate sales business foundation. The caller on the other end of the phone had been presold my services by the referring person. Preselling is what drives my real estate sales business and keeps my client pipeline flowing. If the referral is not in the position to consume my services today, I try to extend other services from my real estate business relationship sphere to meet his or her needs. This leaves the person with the feeling that I wasn't trying to derive an immediate benefit from him or her, thus creating loyalty and building new referrals.

Building confidence in the consumer.

An agent's role is to be a resource and business professional to clients. Being an active listener, being organized, and being proactive affirm clients' decisions in sale or purchase transactions. Being controlling or self-focused is not usually the client's best interest, nor is it perceived as affirming to them. Once clients have trust in your added value, you can make professional suggestions from your real estate sales experience. Keep in mind you have been retained to meet the client's objectives and to affirm his or her decisions in the process. A client can easily choose a different real estate service professional if he or she isn't confident with you.

Looking your best gets you noticed.

As a real estate sales agent, you must attract clients to your services. Therefore, you need to think about your personal packaging and what it communicates to potential clients. Positioning yourself with your appearance, auto, ethics, and business skills is a marketing issue. Consider carefully how to send the right verbal and nonverbal messages to your clients about how you run your real estate sales business.

> Mark's story:
>
> I once met a real estate sales agent who used the fashion statement of wearing hats so the public remembered her as "the hat lady." I laughed to myself and thought, you've got to be kidding! As a client once said to me after we ran into the "hat lady," "Doesn't that agent want to be remembered for what's inside of her head rather than what's on top of it?" I would think so, but maybe those hats were the only marketing tool she thought she had going for her!

Media available for marketing your real estate sales business.

Print

Newspaper: Display ads with photos of your listings, display ads featuring your business, classified ads for your business, and listings are effective and low-cost. Consider sponsoring a real estate column with questions and answers for consumers in your local newspaper.

Magazines: Local and regional magazines are a good way for relocation consumers to find you. The home magazines that are distributed to local businesses are effective for promoting listings.

Cultural events: Concert, theater, and art show programs are a good way to reach a targeted audience for your services.

Church and school bulletins: You can build or affirm your presence in these institutions by promoting your real estate sales business.

Specialized directories: You should utilize yellow or pink page directories focusing on a specific market niche or profile.

Telephone books: You can use this option to increase overall visibility of your real estate sales business.

State association/local Board of REALTORS® publications: These are a great way to build visibility and drive agent-to-agent referral business.

Promotional materials

Some agents use calendars, pens, refrigerator magnets, yardsticks, and so on, to display their real estate business information. An effective leave-behind or direct mail marketing device for existing or potential new clients.

The Internet

Use of the Internet in real estate sales is here to stay. You should keep in mind some fundamentals about Internet consumers. First, they like the anonymity that protects them from unwanted interaction. Second, they like to be in control of communication and keep it impersonal. Third, they appreciate the fact that the Internet provides them with information so they become better educated and can shop more efficiently.

Your company web site: Make sure your current agent profile, your e-mail address, and your telephone extension or direct line are on your agent page within your brokerage site.

Realtor.com: This is a national web site for real estate listings and real estate sales agents. Purchase your own web page here so clients shopping for a real estate sales agent in your market can find you.

You own web site: This is a must-have for all agents. Once your site is set up, it can move with you if you change broker affiliations. You should develop content for your personal web site to provide information and resources for potential clients. Have your web site seeded in the top search engines and enjoy the 24/7 advertising for your real estate sales business. Most web site developers are technology-based. Consider having a visual designer create the graphic design for your site. Uninteresting online brochures do not attract potential clients, so think through the design. Visit web sites and get a feel for what the public is viewing.

Web Site Content Ideas

- About you: Real estate professional profile
- Contact information: E-mail address and link, phone numbers, fax numbers, and brokerage name and address
- List of areas or communities you serve
- Testimonials from clients, active or sold
- Market weather information, including monthly highs and lows
- School information in your market
- Sign-up to be on mailing list
- Links to home-finding sites
- Process in selling a home in your market
- Process in purchasing a home in your market
- Relocation-specific information for your market
- A map-finding link for visualizing the geography of your market
- Your listings
- Niche information if you are marketing to one
- Site map
- Community information
- Information about sports events, cultural events, tourist attractions, and so on

Radio

In some markets, it is cost effective to run ads and host agent-sponsored question-and-answer call-in shows where you discuss the real estate market locally, regionally, and nationally. I found this medium an effective way to reach many consumers and build my real estate business services with a personal touch.

TV and cable

This medium has been very successful for brokerages advertising listings on "home shows." Find out if you can add a tag line about your real estate sales business to listings that appear on your brokerage TV or cable home show. If you can find affordable rates, you might consider hosting your own real estate show as a resource to consumers in your market.

Direct mail

Postcard programs: Several options are available to you. Predesigned postcards with your real estate sales agent business information added can have seasonal messages, kitchen recipes, or current listings printed on the front. Just-sold postcards, with the sold property featured, are popular. These show you are active in the market. Consider mailing postcards to other agents in your market, letting them know when a new listing of yours comes on the market. I also use postcard programs sent to other real estate sales agents to build out-of-market relocation referrals.

Newsletters: Like postcard program, you can send predesigned newsletters to clients. I have also created quarterly and monthly newsletters for clients that give specific information on their micromarket or market niche. Consumers like newsletters that include market statistics and other local news. Be creative!

Word of mouth

The most effective and most cost-efficient form of real estate sales advertising for your new real estate sales business is word of mouth. Serve your clients well and this form of marketing will kick in and help fill your client pipeline.

Cold calling

This telemarketing format works for some agents. I have found relationship building using good time management to be a more effective way of keeping my client pipeline flowing. You do need to develop cold-calling skills so you can be successful contacting referral clients the first time. Cold-calling skills are something your mentor or coach can help you develop. Picking up a phone book or cross directory and cold calling is one of the most difficult types of sales work. Cold calling also has one of the lowest response rates in real estate sales marketing.

Floor Duty

Most real estate sales offices have a monthly schedule of blocks of times for which agents can sign up to take incoming calls from real estate consumers. Consumers are responding to an advertisement or a yard sign of one of your office listings. These calls are a cost-effective way for agents to prospect for new clients. There is an art to managing floor calls, and you should listen to how high-end producers in your office handle them. Practice role-playing floor calls with other new agents to learn how to gather information and presell your real estate abilities to the stranger on the other end of the phone who has a real estate need.

Sample Letter for Floor Call Follow-Up

(current date)

Ms. or Mr. Caller
123 Main Street
Any Town, OH 44444

Dear Ms. or Mr. Caller:

Thank you for contacting our office to inquire about the property for sale on Prospect Avenue.

Enclosed is the information on that property, along with several other properties that offer similar features. Also included is a current map of the area, which I hope will be of use to you in selecting your preferred neighborhood. Please call me if you have questions about any of these homes or if you would like to schedule an appointment to see them or other properties.

As I indicated during our conversation, not all homes for sale are advertised, and I can certainly alert you to other properties as they become available. I will be a happy to assist you throughout your home-buying process, and I look forward to the opportunity of meeting you in the near future.

Sincerely,

Rachael or Ralph Realtor
REALTOR® Associate (Title)

Enclosure

Farming

Farming is traditional method used by real estate sales agents. This is a form of direct mail marketing to consumers in a geographically specific area. Professionals refer to this as one's "farm." If you consider how many agents in your market are farming to the same geographic area, your farming program should be different, creative, and consumer-driven — and should not end up in the consumer's recycling bin with most of the other real estate direct mail pieces!

Volunteering in your community.

If you are new to your community or market, consider volunteering for a nonprofit organization that interests you. You will gradually build visibility in this organization for your real estate sales business and possibly build relationships with future clients.

Public open houses.

Public open houses are inexpensive and are an effective way for you to build visibility with the public. Although a low percentage of homes are sold during public open houses, open houses are a productive prospecting tool for real estate sales agents. Open houses are a way for you to mingle with prospective buyers in your market. Ask buyers attending your open houses if they have an agent. If not, try to build rapport with them and follow up with a call, an e-mail, or letter. Talk to your mentor or managing broker about how to use public open houses as an effective marketing tool.

Business-to-business marketing.

Marketing directly with letters and phone calls to housing offices at colleges and universities, corporate human resource offices, and other businesses that have a supply of new people relocating into your market is an effective way to build a real estate sales business. I have built relationships with rental housing businesses and received referrals of their clients who decided they would rather purchase. Marketing to other real estate transaction service providers such as attorneys, mortgage brokers, appraisers, and inspectors is another good source of referrals.

Agent-to-agent marketing.

Developing a postcard program to market quarterly to other real estate sales agents, regionally or nationally, for their referral business is an effective tool. When attending trade seminars, conferences, and relocation meetings, take time to meet and develop relationships with other agents outside of your market so you can build your referral business.

Open House Hosting Tips

- Confirm that the date and time of the open house doesn't conflict with a major holiday, a sporting event, or other events being held in the neighborhood on that day.
- Decide where you'll place your signs. Allow time to put signs in place before the open house.
- Familiarize yourself with other listings and for-sale-by-owner in the neighborhood.
- Encourage sellers to vacate the premises during the open house.
- Have sellers arrange for pets to be away from home during the open house.
- Open drapes and blinds.
- Have fresh flowers or potted blooming plants.
- Advise sellers to put away jewelry, valuables, coin jars, cash, and so on.
- Walk through the home and familiarize yourself with its features.
- Arrive early to get settled before starting time.
- Contact a lender to sit the open house with you and to provide financing information to open house visitors.
- Don't be a chatterbox and don't hover. Greet your visitors but allow them peace and quiet while they tour the home.
- Be honest about the home's features and improvements.
- If your state requires a disclosure form, have it completed and available to visitors. The same applies to local and national fair housing laws.
- Have comparable sales data available.
- Give visitors property information sheets with facts about the home and community.
- Use a sign-in sheet to collect visitors' names, telephone numbers, and e-mail addresses. Follow up with a telephone call, an e-mail, or a handwritten note after the open house.
- Turn off the lights, close the drapes or blinds, and lock up before leaving.

Sample Letter for Open House Visitor Follow-Up

(current date)

Ms. or Mr. Caller
123 Main Street
Any Town, OH 44444

Dear Ms. or Mr. Caller:

Many thanks for stopping at Sunday's open house at 1000 Prospect in Any Town. It was a pleasure meeting you, and I appreciate your time in sharing your potential plans to move to a new home.

Enclosed is information on a number of properties that may be of interest to you. I also included a map of the area for your reference. As a resident of this area myself, I would be pleased to provide you with whatever community and school information you may find valuable in making your home-buying decision.

Please call if you have questions or if you would like to schedule an appointment to see any of the fine homes currently for sale that would meet your needs. I will be happy to assist you throughout your search for a new home and throughout the entire process of a transaction.

Sincerely,

Rachael or Ralph Realtor
REALTOR® Associate (Title)

Enclosure

Mark's story:

Find the time early on in your real estate sales business to build
referral databases of agents out of your market to whom you can
refer clients. The business relationships I have with other agents
around the country have been a great source of pleasure for me in
my real estate sales business. They bring market-particular
customers, stories, and new ideas I can use in my own business.
I know of many experienced agents who only make referrals.
They no longer work with clients directly. Sounds like a retirement
income to me!

Niche market types.

To make those marketing wheels move, here is a list of some
niches for you to consider. Niche marketing is a focused effort that
will bring results if you display a sincere long-term interest in
these clients.

- Young singles
- Young married/partnered
- New families
- Empty nesters
- Seniors
- Elderly transitional
- Employment-based—doctors, police officers, flight attendants,
  and so on
- Working mothers, stay-at-home fathers, and so on
- Clients of differing ethnics/heritages
- Clients with particular interests/hobbies
- Cultural: music, dance, and theater
- Political
- Handicapped/health issues, barrier-free, breast cancer survivors
- Spiritual/religious
- Professionals and their organizations
- Sports-related
- Same-gender singles

- Life transitional, newly widowed, divorced, or those recovering from substance abuse
- Clients new to your area
- Snowbirds, multiclimate homeowners
- Non-profit organizations
- Chamber of Commerce

Mark's story:

I realized early on in my real estate sales business that niche marketing would be an area of specialization for me. I believed the gay and lesbian consumer was overlooked in my market. So I began a specific marketing campaign to target this consumer. It proved to be successful with my creation and sponsorship of Expo 2000, the largest Chicago-area gay/lesbian business and resource marketplace. In 2001, I published the Metropolitan Guide, a business and resource directory for the suburban/urban gay and lesbian consumer. I also host a web site for this loyal consumer niche called GayLesbianOnline.com. You can model your marketing programs to your particular niche using these successful formats. Be creative!

Networking to build your sphere of influence.

Real estate transactions are a vehicle for personalities and relationships to interact. To be a successful part of this transaction, you need to build relationships through networking. Think about all of the relationships you have with different people, and see if there are ways for you to professionally network these relationships. Consider your spouse's or partner's professional and personal sphere of influence. Your closed and existing client spheres should have potential clients available for your real estate sales business. Social acquaintances, neighbors, service providers, fellow board or committee members, children's contacts, and relatives are available for you to consider.

Chapter 5 Take-Away:

- **Positioning yourself as a market resource to build consumer confidence**
- **Finding niche market types that fit your real estate business**
- **Researching media types for marketing your real estate business**
- **Marketing your business skills versus listing based marketing**

NOTES:

Chapter 6

Keys to the Kingdom

The Home Purchase/Sale Process from Start to Closing

Put your best face forward with clients.

DO:
- Dress professionally. Your style should reflect your market.
- Treat others as you would like to be treated.
- Avoid strong perfumes, colognes, aftershave lotions, and tobacco.
- Listen in an active manner to your clients. Eye contact is important, but staring is unsettling.
- Keep your office organized. New clients will form impressions in the first seconds they meet you and see your office.
- Respect other cultures and lifestyles. (Fair housing laws govern real estate sales agents.) Think before you talk; it could be an expensive comment!
- Follow up, follow up, and follow up.
- Return phone calls and e-mails in a timely manner (within 24 hours).
- Use breath mints.
- Limit or omit cell phone use when with clients.
- Answer your phone in a professional manner.
- Respect your clients' time.
- Be on time for appointments.
- Apologize whether clients are correct or incorrect.
- Learn from every situation.
- Keep conversations with clients focused.
- Know where you're driving. Map-finding web sites are great!
- If you need glasses/contacts or hearing aids, wear them.
- Have a pen and paper handy.
- Have business cards handy.
- Stay calm when your clients are emotional.
- Drive defensively.

DON'T:

- Discuss religion or politics.
- Gossip about your clients, listings, or potential customers.
- Let your hair turn off your clients. Lose that dated style or comb over.
- Use your car as a mobile storage locker. Keep the interior and exterior clean and odor free.
- Interrupt your clients.
- Swear.
- Pretend to know about communities and/or housing styles about which you know nothing.
- Yell at your clients.
- Keep your emotions in check when your clients haven't.
- Discriminate. Keep updated on fair housing.
- Overpromise.
- Lie, cheat, or steal from your clients.

Sample Client Information Sheet

Date:

Her name:

His name:

Address:

Home phone:

Home fax:

Home e-mail:

Her work phone:

His work phone:

Her cell phone:

His cell phone:

Her work fax:

His work fax:

Her work e-mail:

His work e-mail:

Apartment   Condo   Townhouse   House

Pets: Cats   Dogs   Weight:

Rental   Buyer   Seller

Price range:

Parking: Street   Garage   Off-street space

Style: Type: New Construction Rehab   Open

Bedrooms: 1 2 3 4 5 Baths: 1 1$^{1}/_{2}$ 2 2$^{1}/_{2}$ 3 3$^{1}/_{2}$

Relocation: Yes No Referral Fee Due: ____% Relo Coordinator Info:

Connecting with your potential new purchase clients.

You have worked hard to get the potential purchase client to call or
e-mail you. Your first several contacts with this person will be a
different and important phase in your real estate sales business
plan. Your goal now is to create a confidence level in your client.
He or she must be confident of your professional abilities. Start a
file on new clients, and include basic client information, such as
date of first contact; first work-with date; phone, pager, cell phone,
and fax numbers; e-mail address; relocation coordinator information; and referral information.

Mark's story:

Pick up the phone and call those potential new clients you met at
your public open house this last weekend! People don't bite. They
might say no, but you should get used to some rejection and
develop the ability to move forward if you are going to be
successful in real estate sales. A business associate of mine said
early in his career that he would rather chew glass than cold-call.
I'm not the world's greatest cold caller, but I did find other ways to
build a successful business and build relationships. Yes, even with
relationship building, there are first calls, but not always a direct
pitch for business. Reply to e-mail and voice mail in a timely
manner, and you will be perceived as proactive. People like that.

Working with purchase clients.

With new-purchase clients, you are assisting them in establishing
or fine-tuning their purchase parameters. Purchase clients can have
finite or loose parameters. If their parameters are finite, listen
carefully. If clients are merely looking for a resource and service
provider, they will drive their own search. If they come to you with
loose parameters, they most likely are looking for your expertise in
the market as well as your resources and services. The key is

listening. No two clients have the same parameters or personal real estate history.

Purchasers' price range and mortgage.

You must establish clients' parameters in their new home search early in your relationship with them. You need to determine their price range. Your clients probably have a good idea of the home they want and what they are comfortable spending. You need to qualify this price range by suggesting that they get prequalified or preapproved by the mortgage loan provider of their choice or that they select a loan provider from a list that you or your office provides. The mortgage loan officer or broker will provide your clients with a written letter stating the amount and terms of the mortgage. You should ask your clients or the mortgage contact if you can have a copy of the prequalification or approval letter. You will need to present it with a client's contract.

Purchasers' home location, type, size, and style needs.

Clients' home search parameters probably include their choice of community or the location within the community they want to live and the type of home. Do your clients want a condominium, cooperative apartment, single-family home, town house, or manufactured home? (See a list of housing types in the Glossary at the back of the book.) Is the home their primary residence or a second or seasonal home? Buyer considerations include the number of rooms, type of rooms, layout of rooms, location of rooms, number of bedrooms, number of baths, master bath, type of floors and fireplaces. Exterior needs include garage or parking requirements; yard, garden, or lot size; outdoor fencing and lot location, such as corner, interior, or cul-de-sac. Other considerations are proximity to public transportation, shops, schools, and parks, wooded or waterfront lot, size of and view from lot, proximity to golf course, and proximity to town or country.

The desired age of the home is usually determined from the beginning of the purchasing process. Will clients want property that is new, one to ten years old, post-World War II, prewar, or early 1900s? Some clients want contemporary or new homes, some clients want charming old homes, and some clients want a home somewhere in between.

The style of the home is also important. Most clients have a visual idea of how they want their new home to present to the public, its curb appeal. A broad range of styles exist throughout the country. You should first become familiar with those in your market and later familiarize yourself with other popular relocation markets. (See the home style section at the back of this book.)

Condition of the home is another consideration. Some clients lead busy lives and want something that is in excellent condition. Some clients are happy with functional but outdated homes, while others love the project of a fixer upper. Find out what your clients want.

The timeline for a client's purchase should be established at this point. Timelines vary with every client. Having a good sense for what a particular client expects will make you more proactive to his or her needs. It will also allow you to manage your real estate sales business more efficiently.

Showing purchase clients the homes that meet their needs.

After you and your clients have established their home parameters, it is time for you to begin showing them potential new homes. This process varies depending on the volume of properties your clients want to see, available properties in the market, and the process in your market. Depending on the purchase client type, first-time buyer or seasoned real estate repeat buyer, the quantity of homes shown will vary. I've shown just 1 home to purchasers and as many as 122. Most of my clients fall in the 8-18 range. Talk to your mentor or managing broker about how to determine the number of homes to show to purchase clients. After your clients have decided on one or two properties, they will most likely return for another look. Sometimes they'll ask family members, friends, or advisers to come along.

The purchase client makes an offer.

Your clients have found their home and are ready to write an offer. Since this process varies from market to market, I suggest having a thorough discussion and hands-on meeting with your managing broker and mentor on the contractual documents in your state and market. You must have a complete understanding of this process before you go out with your first purchase clients. Practice completing the required documents several times before you sit down with clients. Make sure you are comfortable with the documents. You need to show confidence in the transaction and your abilities when you are face to face with your clients. This is an important time in your new real estate sales business.

Example:
- The seller will accept the terms = contract.
- The seller will change the terms = counteroffer.
- The seller will reject the terms = the end; start over.

Negotiating the offer to purchase.

There are many scenarios at this important stage of your real estate sales business. You should have your mentor or managing broker on standby when you go into this part of the process. Make good use of their expertise. You need to have already discussed negotiating contracts with your mentor or managing broker before you are in the negotiation stage in any contract. Many factors are involved and practices vary from market to market.

Preparing buyers to make an offer.

The big moment has arrived for your clients; they want to write an offer. You have worked many hours for your clients to reach this point. Do not push any buyers into writing an offer if they do not want to. Client confidence is key in real estate sales. Some additional tips:

- Educate your buyers on the offer process. Prepare a chronology of events.
- Prequalify your buyers using a reputable mortgage lender.
- Don't let your personal preferences prejudice you against a home.
- Listen to your buyer's objections.
- Let buyers voice their concerns.
- Help buyers visualize themselves in the home.
- Make sure all the decision makers (parents, spouses, and so on) are available.
- Give buyers time to think over and assimilate what they've seen.
- Don't overwhelm buyers with unnecessary information or talk.
- Ask for the offer!

How to win with your buyers in a multiple offer.

Your clients have fallen in love with their dream home, and so have one or more other buyers! Multiple bids on a single property bring a competitive air to negotiations. Know when to counsel your clients to withdraw from a multiple offer if you feel the dynamic is not in their best interest. Some buyers want to win the multiple offer competition but have remorse the next day. They won, but boy do they feel they over paid! Some tips to clean up an offer.

- Do not ever suggest that your clients remove an attorney approval contingency without consulting an attorney.
- Be flexible with move-in and closing dates.

- Provide mortgage commitment in place of preapproval with offer.
- Have limited contingencies.
- Provide substantial earnest money.
- Have your buyers write a letter to the sellers explaining why they love the seller's home. It works!

Counteroffer Tips

After your initial offer is presented, the seller might accept it or present a counteroffer to it. This process is where good negotiation skills come into use. I would suggest early in your career that you role-play with an experienced agent on overcoming objections and good ethical counteroffer strategies.

- Do not let disagreement over a minor issue take the focus away from an overall good offer.
- Counteroffering is not tennis. Keep unnecessary back-and-forth counteroffers to a minimum.
- Use "my clients need to sleep on it" to diffuse difficult negotiations.
- Explore options to unacceptable terms.
- If your clients don't feel comfortable, they should withdraw.

Your buyer's offer is accepted.

Congratulations! The experience may have been pleasurable, amicable, or frustrating. But the object has been achieved; you have helped your clients accomplish what they set out to do.

After acceptance of your offer with your purchase clients.

The first seven to ten days after acceptance are a busy period for all parties to the contract. Home inspections happen and can include the general mechanical and structural home and property components as well as additional inspections for radon, lead, pests, mold, and buried oil and gas tanks. You should ask your mentor or managing broker what is customary in your market. You should also recommend to your clients that they make sure all necessary inspections are completed. At this time, your clients are working on applications to secure a mortgage. The required documents for the transaction are forwarded to attorneys, escrow companies, mortgage loan companies, appraisers, and (if applicable) relocation companies. You need to find out what is customary in your state and market for the completion of this important document process.

The time between contract and closing or escrow with your purchase clients.

This time can be busy or slow depending on each contract dynamic. Review with your mentor or managing broker your transaction file to make sure you are fulfilling your role in the transaction. Clients do not like surprises. Keep a list with timelines and deadlines and names of those responsible for meeting them. If you believe something is not moving along as it should be, do not assume that no news is good news. Call the transaction participants to be sure the transaction is being completed according to the terms of the contract. This follow-up is vital and it's your responsibility. Check with your mentor or managing broker about the legal responsibilities you and your clients have in this phase of the transaction.

Closing on the transaction with your purchase clients.

All of the administrative work is complete, and the transaction is going to closing or escrow depending on what is common in your market. Have a discussion with your mentor or managing broker before your first closing or escrow to determine your role in this final stage. Congratulations!

The follow-up after closing or escrow.

After closing or escrow, call your clients, and thank them for their business, and offer additional assistance. If you like, you can send, deliver, or bring to closing or escrow a house-warming gift. Ask your mentor or managing broker what is customary. Following up with your closed clients on a regular basis by phone, e-mail, or mail is a good way to remind your clients that you are available to them or their referrals.

Your first contact with a home sale client.

You have spent a lot of time and expense to receive the phone call or e-mail inviting you to your potential home sale client's property. Most home sellers want to discuss in person the need to place their home on the market. Many factors impact this decision, including downsizing, an upsizing, relocation, marriage, divorce, death, a life transition, children, a move to a nursing home, retirement, and a consolidation of extended family. It is important to find out what is motivating your potential new home sale client to sell. Your first visit to a client's home might be to get aquainted, to tour the property, and to establish an initial positioning of your professional skills.

Some sellers are all business and want only one visit to accomplish everything, including the presentation of your comparative market analysis (CMA). The CMA is your professional market-based opinion of how the seller's property should be positioned with regard to price and marketing. The CMA also includes information on active, pending, and sold comparable properties and profes-sional information about you and your company. The CMA can also include custom features unique to the property. Your mentor is an important resource for building a successful CMA. The CMA tool is one of the cornerstones of a successful real estate sales business.

In most cases, the seller invites several real estate professionals to the property to interview them and hear their opinions on value and marketing. Some of these agents may be from your office or company. Ask your managing broker what your company policy is on this situation. Competition is tough in most markets for aquiring listings of properties by sellers. List price, commission rates, marketing, real estate sales agent professional history, and personality compatibility are factors sellers consider when choosing a real estate sales agent to represent their property.

Mark's story:

Your first meeting with new potential listing clients can be a tense experience for them. Be relaxed, focused, and on time. Try to put your clients at ease by being natural and honest. I admit when I don't know an answer, but I find it and get back to the client. I am professional at listing appointments and do not bad-mouth the competition, even if one of them has placed some doubt about my company in the client's mind. Real estate is a competitive business, but negative competitive comments are unprofessional and may cost you a listing!

The home sale listing agreement.

Congratulations on your first home sale listing and client! Your new real estate sales business is off to a great start. The actual document format for listing a home varies by state and real estate company. Before you go on a listing appointment, ask your mentor or managing broker to review your company's listing agreement and required federal, state, and local disclosures. Ask him or her to review what makes a legal and enforceable listing agreement in your state.

Putting your new home sale listing on market.

Once you have completed the listing agreement and disclosures, your new listing is ready for presentation on the market. Ask your mentor what steps are typical to get your new listing marketed by your company, by your own real estate sales business, and by multiple listing or other listing services. Typically, many systems and customs affect how you market your listing. Take the time to research, test, and use existing and innovative concepts for the successful sale and closing of your listing. The time your new listing is on the market before the first offer is received depends on many market factors as well as your own efforts. Talk to your mentor about what is typical in your market.

Presenting a home purchase offer to your sellers.

You will be pleased when another agent calls with the news of an offer on your listing. Some offers will be great and some will be a real test of your real estate and people skills. The most important thing to remember is not where the offer starts, but where it ends.

- Update your comparable market data on list prices and sale prices.
- Qualify the buyer with details about the down payment and loan prequalifications.
- Be prepared for objections from the seller. Have information needed to respond.
- Calculate bottom line net proceeds for your seller, after expenses.
- Don't disparage the seller's property.
- Don't assume you know who the decision maker is.
- Learn about the personalities of the principals and sales associates with whom you'll be negotiating.
- Cover all aspects of the offer with the seller.
- Let the seller read the contract uninterrupted.

- Go over each paragraph of the offer, explaining what it means and how it can impact the process after acceptance.
- Humanize the buyers. Tell the sellers some details about the buyers.
- Tell the sellers that the buyers love their house!

Receiving a contract on your listing.

You may receive one or more offers on your listing. Your mentor or managing broker can advise you on the steps in your state and market for handling an offer. If you receive multiple offers on a listing, ask your mentor or managing broker what procedures you need to follow.

Counteroffer Tips

- Do not let disagreement over a minor issue take the focus away from an overall good offer.
- Counteroffering is not tennis. Keep unnecessary back-and-forth counteroffers to a minimum.
- Use "my clients need to sleep on it" to diffuse difficult negotiations.
- Explore options to unacceptable terms.
- If your clients don't feel comfortable, they should withdraw.

Tips on handling multiple offers.

- Present all offers promptly.
- Present offers in the order they were submitted.
- Make buyers and their salespersons aware of your procedure for handling multiple offers.
- Provide all parties with the same information.
- Furnish sellers with multiple offer comparison sheets. (See sample at the end of this chapter.)
- Keep everyone informed at all stages of the process.
- Remind losers in a multiple offer that their offer (with their permission) can be used as a back-up offer.

Acceptance of a contract with your home sale clients.

The bringing of an offer to acceptance should be a rewarding experience for you. The first seven to ten days after acceptance are a busy period for all parties to the contract. The potential new purchasers should have a home inspection done. If issues arise as a result of the inspection, you need to communicate these to the sellers or their legal representative. This process varies by state and market; ask your mentor or managing broker what is required in your state. The purchaser's mortgage company most likely will need to complete an appraisal on the property. Your managing broker or mentor can address what is customary in your state and market on the appraisal process for your listing.

The time between contract and closing or escrow with your home sale clients.

This time can be busy or slow depending on each contract dynamic. Review with your mentor or managing broker your transaction file to make sure you are fulfilling your role in the transaction. Clients do not like surprises. Keep a list with timelines and deadlines and names of those responsible for meeting them. If you believe something is not moving along as it should be, do not assume that no news is good news. Call the transaction participants to be sure the transaction is being completed according to the terms of the contract. This follow-up is vital and it's your responsibility. Check with your mentor or managing broker about the legal responsibilities you and your clients have in this phase of the transaction.

Closing on the transaction with your home sale clients.

All of the administrative work is complete, and the transaction is going to closing or escrow depending on what is common in your market. Have a discussion with your mentor or managing broker before your first closing or escrow to determine your role in this final stage. Congratulations!

Home sale client postclosing or escrow follow-up.

After closing or escrow, call your clients, thank them for their business, and offer additional assistance. If you like, you can send, deliver, or bring to closing or escrow a house-warming gift. Ask your mentor or managing broker what is customary. Following up with your closed clients on a regular basis by phone, e-mail, or mail is a good way to remind your clients that you are available to them or their referrals.

Transaction terms you should know.

You should familiarize yourself with processes and terms common in your market and state. Ask your managing broker or mentor about your local transaction process.

Mortgage Participants and Related Terms

Adjustable rate mortgage (ARM): A type of mortgage loan whose interest rate is tied to an economic index, which fluctuates with the market. Typical ARM periods are for one, three, five, and seven years.

Annual percentage rate (APR): The total costs (interest rate, closing costs, fees, and so on.) that are part of a borrower's loan, expressed as a percentage rate of interest. The total costs are amortized over the term of the loan.

Application fees: Fees that mortgage companies charge buyers at the time of written application for a loan; for example, fees for running credit reports of borrowers, property appraisal fees, and lender-specific fees.

Appraisal: A document of opinion of property value at a specific point in time.

Assumable mortgage: One in which the buyer agrees to fulfill the obligations of the existing loan agreement that the seller made with the lender. When assuming a mortgage, a buyer becomes personally liable for the payment of principal and interest. The original mortgagor should receive a written release from the liability when the buyer assumes the original mortgage.

Balloon mortgage: A type of mortgage that is generally paid over a short period of time, but is amortized over a longer period of time. The borrower typically pays a combination of principal and interest. At the end of the loan term, the entire unpaid balance must be repaid.

Conventional mortgage: A type of mortgage that has certain limitations placed on it to meet secondary market guidelines. Mortgage companies, banks, and savings and loans underwrite conventional mortgages.

Credit report: A report that includes the history for a borrower's credit accounts, outstanding debts, and payment timelines on past or current debts.

Credit score: A score assigned to a borrower's credit report based on information contained therein.

Divorce: The legal separation of a husband and wife effected by a court decree that totally dissolves the marriage relationship.

Decree: A judgment of the court that sets out the agreements and rights of the parties.

Down payment: The amount of cash put toward a purchase by the borrower.

Escrow account for real estate taxes and insurance: An account in which borrowers pay monthly prorations for real estate taxes and property insurance.

FHA (Federal Housing Administration) Loan Guarantee: A guarantee by the FHA that a percentage of a loan will be under-written by a mortgage company or bank.

Gift letter: A letter to a lender stating that a gift of cash has been made to the buyer(s) and that the person gifting the cash to the buyer is not expecting the gift to be repaid. The exact wording of the gift letter should be requested of the lender.

Good faith estimate: Under the Real Estate Settlement Procedures Act, within three days of an application submission, lenders are required to provide in writing to potential borrowers a good faith estimate of closing costs.

Hazard insurance: Insurance that covers losses to real estate from damages that might affect its value.

Homeowner's insurance: Coverage that includes personal liability and theft insurance in addition to hazard insurance.

HUD/RESPA (Housing and Urban Development/Real Estate Settlement Procedures Act): A document and statement that details all of the monies paid out and received at a real estate property closing.

Hybrid adjustable rate: Offers a fixed rate the first 5 years and then adjusts annually for the next 25 years.

Interest rate float: When the borrower decides to delay locking the interest rate on his or her loan. The borrower can float the rate in expectation of the rate moving down. At the end of the float period, he or she must lock in a rate.

Interest rate lock: When the borrower and lender agree to lock in a rate on a loan. Terms and conditions can be attached to the lock.

Loan: An amount of money that is lent to a borrower who agrees to repay the amount plus interest.

Loan application: Documents that buyers who are requesting a loan fill out and submit to their lender.

Loan closing costs: The amount of costs a lender charges to close the borrower's loan. These costs vary from lender to lender and market to market.

Loan commitment: A written document telling the borrowers that the mortgage company has agreed to lend them a specific amount of money at a specific interest rate for a specific period of time. The loan commitment may also contain conditions on which the loan commitment is based.

Loan package: The group of mortgage documents the borrower's lender sends to the closing or escrow.

Loan processor: An administrative individual who is assigned to check, verify, and assemble all of the documents and the buyer's funds and the borrower's loan for closing.

Loan underwriter: One who underwrites a loan for another. Some lenders have investors underwrite a buyer's loan.

Mortgage banker: One who lends the bank's funds to borrowers and brings lenders and borrowers together.

Mortgage broker: A business that or an individual who unites lenders and borrowers and processes mortgage applications.

Mortgage loan servicing company: A company that collects monthly mortgage payments from borrowers.

Payoff letter: A written document from a seller's mortgage company stating the amount of money needed to pay a loan in full.

Preapproval: A higher level of buyer/borrower prequalification required by a mortgage lender. Some preapprovals have conditions the borrower must meet.

Prepaid interest: Funds paid by the borrower at closing based on the number of days left in the month of closing.

Prepayment penalty: A fine imposed on the borrower by the lender if the loan is paid off before it comes due.

Prequalification: The process of the mortgage company telling a buyer in advance of the formal mortgage application and how much money the borrower can afford to borrow. Some prequalifications have conditions the borrower must meet.

Principal: The amount of money a buyer borrows.

Principal, interest, taxes, and insurance (PITI): The four parts that make up a borrower's monthly mortgage payment.

Private mortgage insurance (PMI): A special insurance paid by a borrower in monthly installments, typically of loans of more than 80 percent of the value of the property.

Release deed: A written document stating that a seller or buyer has satisfied his or her obligation on a debt. This document is usually recorded.

Secondary market: An institutional investment market that purchases mortgages from mortgage lenders.

VA (Veterans Administration) Loan Guarantee: A guarantees on a mortgage amount backed by the Department of Veterans Affairs.

Will: A document by which a person disposes of his or her property after death.

W-2: The Internal Revenue form issued by employer to employee to reflect compensation and deductions to compensation.

1099: The Internal Revenue form issued to independent contractors to reflect compensation given by the issuer.

Home Inspection Terms

Environmental inspections: Property inspections for, among others, asbestos, radon, urea formaldehyde, lead, and mold. Agents must be familiar with the disclosure and inspection requirements in relation to all types of environmental inspections.

Home inspection: The process that evaluates and reports to the client the condition of the mechanical and structural components of a property. Regulation of home inspectors varies from state to state.

Oil and gas tanks: buried or above grade: Another type of inspection required of some properties.

Pest/Insect: Another type of home inspection.

Septic tank and water well: Inspections required of some properties with private sewer and water.

Structural, mechanical, condition: Inspections that include but are not limited to foundations, roofs, siding, gutters and downspouts, porches and decks, chimneys, fireplaces, windows, doors, plumbing, electrical, heating, air conditioning, appliances, hot water heaters, pools, interior and exterior walls, and concrete and asphalt surfaces.

Additional Transaction Terms

Attorney-at-law: A person licensed by the state to practice law. Duties of a real estate attorney for buyer and seller include: reviewing and discussing contract with client, making recommendations based on a client's objectives, conveying changes or suggestions in writing to other attorney, reviewing and discussing inspection items with client, communicating with other attorney in writing, and attending closing. Duties for just the buyer include: following progress of mortgage; requesting additional time, if necessary, for unconditional commitment; and explaining lender documents and seller documents at closing. Duties for just the seller include: ordering title search, survey, and, if property is a condo, certain condominium papers, as well as payoff letter, and preparing all documents to transfer title. The attorney should communicate with the client regularly regarding all steps in the procedure.

Disclosure documents: All required federal, state, county, and city disclosure forms that need to be presented to clients and/or signed by clients and agents. It is very important for you to know all the required disclosures that you need to prepare or receive with an offer. Write it down on all your active files until you know it. Disclosure is a large part of you being compliant under your real estate license.

Fill in all required disclosure documents for your transaction files.

Federal:

State:

County:

City:

The following is an agent's checklist of necessary items...

- Blank real estate contracts, disclosures, W-9s
- Business cards
- Blank letterhead and envelopes
- Preapprovals and other client-specific documents
- Copies of active, pending, and sold comparables
- Blank listing agreements and supporting documents
- Required booklets and information for disclosure documents
- Market area maps
- Note paper
- Pens, pencils, and transparent tape
- Signs: open house, for sale, riders, agent name, pending, under contract, new price, sold, open Sunday
- Calculator
- Camera
- Calendar
- Flashlight and batteries
- Tape measure
- Cell phone and beeper
- Laptop computer
- Lockboxes: Supra® (electronic)/combination

Mark's story:

One of the services I offer my clients is lists of professional transaction service providers. When my clients select someone from this list, they can depend on this service provider. Find professional transaction service providers and communicate with them. No news is not necessarily good news in a transaction. No news may mean someone has dropped the ball. If you want to go to closing as the contract states, stay in touch with all transaction participants. Satisfied clients are the best source of referrals.

Escrow: A system whereby a third party receives all funds and documents relating to the transfer of real estate. The transfer is complete when the third party is satisfied that all predetermined requirements have been met.

Title company: An organization that searches recorded documents to determine whether there are defects in the title. After clearing the defects, if any, the title company guarantees clear title to the buyer and lender by issuing the title policy.

Chapter 6 Take-Away:

- Working with purchase clients

- Working with home sale clients

- Understanding the process: contract to closing

- Interacting with transaction participants

NOTES:

Multiple Offer Comparison

Property Address: **Seller:**

NOTE: All real estate contracts are to be presented in their entirety.

	Offer 1	Offer 2	Offer 3
Price			
Inclusions			
Exclusions			
Initial Earnest Money			
Balance Earnest Due			
Reply Deadline			
Mortgage Contingency Commitment Date			
Preapproval Letter?			
Closing Date			
Possession Date			
Rent Back/Escrow			
Closing Date			
Tax Prorations/Unpaid			
House to Sell?			
House Sale to Close?			
Time Frame for Kick Out			
Transfer Stamps Paid By			
Seller Disclosures Signed?			
Lead Paint Disclosure Signed?			
Interest-Bearing Account?			
Inspection: # of Days			
Attorney Approval Days			
Other Provisions			

Negotiating Checklist

Address: _____

Client Name: _____

Client Phone Numbers:
Home: _____Office: _____Cellular: _____
Pager: _____
Co-op Agent: _____
Agent's Phone Numbers:
Home: _____Office: _____
Cellular: _____Pager: _____Fax: _____
Initial Offer: $_____ Date/Time: _____
Counteroffer: $_____ Date/Time: _____
Other Issues:

_____
_____
_____

Counteroffer: $_____Date/Time: _____
Other Issues:_____
_____

Counteroffer: $_____Date/Time: _____
Other Issues:_____
_____

Counteroffer: $_____Date/Time: _____
Other Issues:_____
_____
_____
_____

Date Purchaser Signed: _____ Date Delivered: _____
Date Seller Signed: _____ Date Delivered: _____

Chapter 7

Know Your Community

Who Are Your Coworkers and Your Competition?

Defined below are some brokerage and agent profiles and brokerage styles. Familiarize yourself with them; you will find them useful when starting out in real estate.

Brokerage Profiles

Auction: A brokerage that holds auctions for sellers to market properties to consumers or businesses.

Builder/developer: A brokerage that focuses on new construction or rehabilitation of existing properties. Agents should ask in their first phone call or e-mail to a builder/developer if he or she will cooperate with other brokers on commissions. Typically, agents must register a client on their first visit together to the property or sales center.

Buyer representation only: One that represents only buyers in their market area. Buyers or sellers can compensate a brokerage depending on the brokerage agreement.

Commercial: One that specializes in forms of commercial properties such as office buildings, shopping centers, multifamily buildings, land for development, businesses, and businesses with real estate.

Discount: A lower commission for listings or transaction services compared to brokerage competitors. Discounts appeal to value-driven sellers. Agents can offer full service or limited services in exchange for a lower commission or fees.

Fee for service: A menu-based emerging brokerage format where the consumer contracts for specific services that are part of the transaction process at a fixed rate of compensation. Example: Enter home in multiple listing services for a fee of $750. Host public open house for $100. Negotiate contract for $1,000.

For sale by owner: One that markets directly to sellers selling their own property. Other options include conversion to a fee for service and full-service brokerage.

Franchise: A brokerage that affiliates with a company in exchange for marketing and name recognition.

Independent: One that is not affiliated with any other regional or national company.

Internet/e-commerce: An Internet consumer-based brokerage where the real estate sales agent is provided with sales prospects from the brokerage web site. Typically, the real estate sales agent works from a home office and reports to a regional managing broker.

National: One that affiliates with a company that provides national marketing and name recognition.

Regional: One that affiliates with a company that provides regional marketing and name recognition.

Salaried agents: Licensed real estate sales agents compensated by their broker in the form of a salary instead of a straight commission. The broker receives the commission from all transactions the agent receives, and the broker compensates the agent with a salary. Some brokerages offer a variation where there is an additional bonus of compensation to the agent when the agent meets predetermined sales goals.

Brokerage Styles

Traditional: One that offers consumers full-service transactions. Traditional brokerages represent sellers and buyers in their market area and typically have relocation, mortgage, insurance, and title services available for their clients.

Boutique: A brokerage positioned within a market to appeal to a specific consumer or market profile; i.e., upper-bracket properties, specific developments, or historic properties.

Geography-Based

Urban: One that focuses brokerage marketing on a certain district or property within a larger urban market.

Suburban: One that specializes in certain communities or subdivisions within a suburban market area.

Rural: One that specializes in ranches, farms, agricultural land, or surrounding communities.

Second home/vacation/snowbird: One that markets to out-of-market consumers for second, vacation, or alternative seasonal properties.

Time-share: One that specializes in marketing to a consumer's ownership of a specified time interval in a property.

Agent Profiles

The majority of real estate sales agents are a pleasure to work with. However, you may run into one who frustrates you. Here are some background profiles you may find useful when working with other agents.

Full-time: Agents who take the business seriously and maximize time management. If you find yourself derailed with this agent, good communication skills will move you forward in the transaction.

Part-time: Agents whose other employment, home responsibilities, and activities can impact their communication and focus.

History in real estate sales: Agents who have differing levels of skills and knowledge, and can be either new to the business or those who have been a real estate sales agent for many years. You will find long time agents with outdated information or skills. Be patient with all, and offer professional advice if needed to move you both forward in a transaction.

Mark's story:

At a new listing in a seller's market, I was holding a public open house. I had good traffic through the property. Near the end, an agent came with clients to see the house. The clients liked it and the agent said she would write a contract. She returned shortly and presented an earnest money check and a written offer to me, without disclosures and without a prequalification letter for her buyers. I thanked her for the offer and said I would present it to my seller. I also added that the seller most likely would not respond without supporting documents stating that the buyers had the ability to close a loan for the property and the required signed disclosures. The agent became belligerent and asked whether I knew she had been in real estate sales for 25 years. She went on to say that with her reputation, her clients did not need to provide the seller with documentation of their ability to secure a mortgage for the property. I replied in a professional manner that I did not know her or her clients and that my seller did not know her or her clients, but we would like to pursue her offer if she provided the information necessary to make a decision. The agent said she would get back to me. She did. She provided the information and we went to closing, but not without her continued grandstanding about her experience in real estate sales. Stick to your ethics and ask for required disclosures and documentation.

Previous career: Agents whose professional history can affect how they respond in business situations.

Age: Agents whose age does not matter in their transactions. Attitude and maturity are more likely to impact agents' interactions with each other.

Gender: Agents whose gender doesn't present issues with other agents. Agents should consider gender-specific perspectives when communicating with other real estate sales agents.

Educational background: Agents whose educational background of real estate sales can vary widely. An agent with an MBA is not necessarily more successful than agents without that level of education. Real estate sales is a people business, and not all successful entrepreneurial real estate sales agents are highly educated.

Financial Needs from Real Estate Sales

Sole supporter: One who doesn't have secondary household income to offset compensation irregularities from real estate sales.

Secondary supporter: One who has a partner or spouse who provides primary income to the household and can assist in weathering compensation irregularities from real estate sales.

Where Their Residential Real Estate Sales Business Is Based

Retail professional office: Agents whose professional environment motivates them to work in real estate sales. Some real estate sales agents like the focus and interaction that an office affords them.

Home: Agents whose preference is to be able to multitask at home handling family and household responsibilities and run their real estate sales business. Some agents prefer the privacy of a home office.

Virtual: Agents who may have a temporary desk at their real estate sales office or an office at home. They travel with their handheld organizer and laptop when in the market.

Short/long distance from market: Agents who may live full- or part-time in the market where they have their office. They may live a short distance from the office or work removed from their market in a second home.

Chapter 7 Take-Away:

- **Understanding various brokerage profiles**

- **Realizing that agent profiles differ, depending on agent perspective of real estate sales**

NOTES:

Chapter 8

A Moving Experience?

Relocation: What's It All About and Is It for You?

What's it all about?

Relocation is the process of transferring a current or new employee from one geographic location to another. Transfers result from an employee's promotion or request or from an employer's reorganization, such as one employer purchasing another employer, causing workforce consolidation. Relocation companies are retained by an employee's company to organize some or all of the transferee's (employee's) move. The relocation company is referred to as the third-party company; the employer and transferee are Parties 1 and 2. Many financial aspects of the relocation process are designed to shift income tax issues from the transferee to the employer.

Two aspects of the transferee's relocation need coordination. First, the current home, if owned, needs to be placed on the real estate market. Real estate agents, movers, and service companies are brought in to bid on the work required to prepare the transferee's property for market. Second is the purchase or rental of the transferee's home in the new location. This process includes familiarization trips, market overviews, home purchase or lease, school searches, trailing spouse's (the employee's spouse or partner) needs, temporary housing, storage of household goods, and the mortgage application for the new purchase. International transferee's bring an additional set of needs to the relocation process.

The business of relocation and your role.

The relocation company is a business, and it is in business to keep its clients, the employer, and the transferee satisfied. This should be your perspective throughout your business relationship with the relocation company. As the home sale or purchase agent, you and your brokerage are a vendor to the relocation company. The person with whom you interact at the transferee's relocation company is the relocation coordinator. The relocation coordinator orchestrates

the transferee's move. Often the coordinator is in a regional or national office with limited knowledge of your market conditions or customs. For this reason, he or she contracts with your company and you to represent his or her client. The relocation coordinator has multiple transferees, just as you have multiple clients. The relocation process is a potentially stressful time for the transferee, juggling current home, job position, family, and pets. In addition to the current home and all of the decisions that must be made at the new destination is the added stress of commuting to the new job. The nature of the relocation process might make you, the real estate sales agent, the only relocation professional with whom the transferee works directly. Being on the first line of assistance can be challenging for a new real estate sales agent.

One major distinction in the relocation process is that you have clients in addition to the transferee. In the background are the employer; the third-party relocation coordinator; and, if your company has an in-house relocation department, this relocation representative as well. Each person will impact the process for your client, the transferee. The relocation coordinator(s) and employer are your support system. By communicating regularly and professionally to develop a business relationship with them, future relocation business will be referred to you.

Working effectively with your clients in the dynamics of their relocation.

The first-time transferee: Relocation is a process. Many first-time transferees are overwhelmed by all of the decisions they need to make. Being understanding and listening is an effective way to help them manage the process. Do what is expected of you professionally. If they need something you can't provide, don't be afraid to refer them back to their relocation coordinator, to their relocation policy, or to their new supervisor or human resources department.

The seasoned transferee: Usually, seasoned transferees know the overview of the relocation process. Occasionally some of the benefits in their relocation policy have been revised since their last relocation and can be a source of surprise if they haven't read the policy. Understand that relocating can be difficult even for the seasoned transferee. You might experience transferees coming in and out of your market in shorter periods of time. Building a professional relationship with them when they're coming into the market can solidify your working with them when they are leaving the market.

The trailing spouse: Patience is the rule of thumb with the first-time or seasoned trailing spouse or partner. They typically have many needs and questions that require your assistance. Often the trailing spouse orchestrates most of the day-to-day personal aspects of the relocation. Their own employment issues may be an additional concern or priority. Recognize that the first weeks in a new home, after the spouse or partner has left for work and the children have left for school, can be isolating for trailing spouses. Offer your assistance at this transitional time.

The children: The ages of a transferee's children will impact their reaction to the move. Younger children move easily as long as their parents are supportive in the transition. Older children with long-term friendships can be insecure about establishing new friendships. Take the lead from your clients in addressing their children's needs. Don't assume seasoned transferees' children will react to another relocation the same way they did the previous relocation.

The international transferee: The international transferee brings additional needs to the relocation. Cultural, religious, or ethnic transitioning may be a concern. Be sensitive to these issues. In addition to housing needs, you may also be asked about applying for a driver's license, a social security number, or an identification numbers and about finding ethnic or English schools. Some trailing spouses need new employment visas.

The paperwork involved in the relocation process.

You must like paperwork to do relocation business. Your clients may have thought you did a great job finding them the right home, but if you didn't submit your paperwork to the necessary parties in a timely and professional manner, you may not receive additional referrals. As they say in the relocation business, "You're as good as your last referral!"

The types of paperwork vary according to which side of the relocation is involved. Both sides require submitting supporting documentation of the transferee's progress throughout the relocation process. Early in your real estate sales career take a relocation course offered by your relocation department or become relocation certified by a national relocation company or organization.

Referral fees are part of relocation.

Early in your real estate sales career as you pursue relocation business as part of your business plan, you will hear comments from experienced agents about relocation. Some agents can't understand why you would pay part of your commission back to the third-party relocation company for the piece of business you received from them. The same agents have a perspective that with the paperwork involved in working with relocation clients, you should be paid more! If relocation is part of your business plan, go ahead and pursue relocation business, and watch your sales volume and ancillary referral business, grow. You will pay relocation referral fees on home sales or purchases of 20 to 45 percent of your commission. Eighty to 55 percent of something is better than 80 to 55 percent of nothing!

Is relocation for you?

Only you know whether relocation works in your business plan. To do relocation business over the long term, you may find you need the following skills:

- Making professional presentations and communicating well
- Listening effectively and assimilating your client's needs and how they fit into the market
- Being patient and understanding to allow your clients to become educated about the market until they have the confidence in you and your market to make a commitment to housing
- Being organized to track many aspects of each relocation transaction
- Actualizing your business plan so you can benefit from the ongoing supply of transferees moving in and out of the market
- Pursuing the financial opportunities of relocation and what they can add to your new real estate sales business
- Being able to make people feel at home in your market

Chapter 8 Take-Away:

- **Understanding the business of relocation**

- **Understaning transferee types**

- **Implementing the process, paperwork, and referral fees of relocation**

Relocation Glossary

Amended value: The actual sale price after the seller successfully markets and sells his or her home through the broker of his or her choice. The sale is turned over to a third-party relocation company for closing, and the guaranteed offer is amended or changed.

Appraised price (AP): The price the third-party relocation company offers (under most contracts) the seller for his or her property. Generally, the average of two or more independent appraisals.

Broker's market analysis (BMA): The real estate broker's opinion of the expected final net sale price, determined after acquisition of the property by the third-party company.

Broker's price opinion (BPO): The real estate broker's opinion of the expected final net sale price, determined prior to the acquisition of the property.

Competitive/comparative market analysis (CMA): The analysis used to provide market information to the seller and assist the real estate broker in securing the listing.

Carrying costs: Cost incurred to maintain a property (taxes, interest, insurance, utilities, and so on).

Corporate client: The company with whom the third-party relocation company has an agreement to handle the relocating employees.

Contract of sale: The agreement between the third-party relocation company and the seller (transferee) whereby the third-party company purchases the property owned by the seller.

Destination services: Services provided to the transferee at the new location. They can include familarization tours, temporary housing, school searches, and so on.

Direct home selling costs (DHSC): Carrying costs, loss on sale, repairs and improvements, commission, closing costs, principal, interest, taxes and insurance, interest on equity loans, and utilities.

DOM: Days on market.

Gross sale price: The sale price before any concessions.

Guaranteed offer: The amount, after appraisals, the employer offers the transferring employee for his or her property.

Home-finding assistance: Additional assistance provided by a third-party relocation company that can include information about the destination community.

Inspection rider: A rider to the purchase agreement between the third-party relocation company and the buyer of the transferee's property stating that property is being sold "as is." All inspection reports conducted by the third-party company are disclosed to the buyer, and it is the buyer's duty to do his or her own inspections and tests.

Inventory: A transferee's property the third-party relocation company has acquired.

List date: The actual date the property was listed with the current broker.

List price: The current list price of the property.

Listing exclusion: A clause included in the listing agreement when the seller (transferee) lists his or her property with a broker.

Market familiarization trip: A visit by the transferee to the new location to view housing market options and location highlights.

Marketing period: The period of time in which the transferee may market his or her property (typically 45, 60, or 90 days) as directed by the third-party company's contract with the employer.

Net sales price: Gross sales price minus concessions to the buyers.

Property or home-finding assistance status reports: Reports filed weekly or monthly by the listing or buying agent representing the transferee.

R & I: Estimated and actual repair and improvement costs.

Relist: Property that was listed with another broker but relisted with the current broker.

Temporary housing: Housing that the transferee occupies until permanent housing is selected or becomes available.

Third-party company: A relocation company hired by the employee's employer to coordinate the employee's move to a new location.

Trailing spouse: The spouse or partner of the employee being moved to a new location by an employer.

Transaction management fee (TMF): A fee charged by listing brokers to the seller as part of the listing agreement.

Vacate date: The date on which the seller (transferee) vacates the property (generally the date when responsibility for property expenses by the transferee ends) and the third-party company assumes ownership for the property through a buyout.

Chapter 9

Understanding the Terms

Real Estate Sales Office Glossary and Agent Security

Real Estate Sales Agent Security and Safety

Talk to your managing broker or mentor about how you can take steps to avoid situations where your personal safety is at risk on the job. I have included ideas to help you with new clients or walk-ins at your office who want to view property right away. First, trust yourself. If you feel uncomfortable with the person, ask for and photocopy his or her identification and leave the copy with your front-desk staff before you take the clients on a property tour. You can also ask another agent to accompany you. Don't be reluctant to ask for assistance from another agent. I would recommend meeting all first-time clients at your real estate sales office before showing properties to them. If you feel uncomfortable having strangers in your car, you can take separate cars. To avoid surprises at property showings, ring the bell, knock, and announce youself just inside the door. An announcement upon entry can prevent embarrassing situations.

Public open houses pose different security issues. If you feel uncomfortable hosting the open house by yourself, ask another agent to cohost. Keep your cell phone ready with emergency numbers preprogrammed as an additional safety measure.

Remember, your personal safety is more important than the amount of lost compensation from a potential transaction. If you ever feel uncomfortable with clients, trust yourself and remove yourself from the situation as quickly as possible. Think smart, pay attention to your surroundings, and have a safety plan in mind in case of threatening behavior.

Another important issue is dealing with pets at property showings. If you or your clients are pet lovers, you bring a different perspective to cats and dogs than nonpet lovers. Allergies may be a consideration. Be sensitive to a client's perspective on pets.

Glossary

1031 exchange or Starker exchange: The delayed exchange of properties that qualifies for tax purposes as a tax-deferred exchange.

1099: The statement of income reported to the IRS for an independent contractor.

A/I: A contract that is pending with attorney and inspection contingencies.

Accompanied showings: Those showings where the listing agent must accompany an agent and his or her clients when viewing a listing.

Addendum: An addition to; a document.

Adjustable rate mortgage (ARM): A type of mortgage loan whose interest rate is tied to an economic index, which fluctuates with the market. Typical ARM periods are one, three, five, and seven years.

Agent: The licensed real estate salesperson or broker who represents buyers or sellers.

Amended value: The actual sale price after the seller successfully markets and sells his or her home through the broker of his or her choice. The sale is turned over to a third-party relocation company for closing, and the guaranteed offer is amended or changed.

Annual percentage rate (APR): The total costs (interest rate, closing costs, fees, and so on) that are part of a borrower's loan, expressed as a percentage rate of interest. The total costs are amortized over the term of the loan.

Application fees: Fees that mortgage companies charge buyers at the time of written application for a loan; for example, fees for running credit reports of borrowers, property appraisal fees, and lender-specific fees.

Appointments: Those times or time periods an agent shows properties to clients.

Appraisal: A document of opinion of property value at a specific point in time.

Appraised price (AP): The price the third-party relocation company offers (under most contracts) the seller for his or her property. Generally, the average of two or more independent appraisals.

"As-is": A contract or offer clause stating that the seller will not repair or correct any problems with the property. Also used in listings and marketing materials.

Assumable mortgage: One in which the buyer agrees to fulfill the obligations of the existing loan agreement that the seller made with the lender. When assuming a mortgage, a buyer becomes personally liable for the payment of principal and interest. The original mortgagor should receive a written release from the liability when the buyer assumes the original mortgage.

Back on market (BOM): When a property or listing is placed back on the market after being removed from the market recently.

Back-up agent: A licensed agent who works with clients when their agent is unavailable.

Balloon mortgage: A type of mortgage that is generally paid over a short period of time, but is amortized over a longer period of time. The borrower typically pays a combination of principal and interest. At the end of the loan term, the entire unpaid balance must be repaid.

Back-up offer: When an offer is accepted contingent on the fall through or voiding of an accepted first offer on a property.

Bill of sale: Transfers title to personal property in a transaction.

Board of REALTORS® (local): An association of REALTORS® in a specific geographic area.

Broker: A state licensed individual who acts as the agent for the seller or buyer.

Broker of record: The person registered with his or her state licensing authority as the managing broker of a specific real estate sales office.

Broker's market analysis (BMA): The real estate broker's opinion of the expected final net sale price, determined after acquisition of the property by the third-party company.

Broker's price opinion (BPO): The real estate broker's opinion of the expected final net sale price, determined prior to the acquisition of the property.

Broker's tour: A preset time and day when real estate sales agents can view listings by multiple brokerages in the market.

Buyer: The purchaser of a property.

Buyer agency: A real estate broker retained by the buyer who has a fiduciary duty to the buyer.

Buyer agent: The agent who shows the buyer's property, negotiates the contract or offer for the buyer, and works with the buyer to close the transaction.

Carrying costs: Cost incurred to maintain a property (taxes, interest, insurance, utilities, and so on).

Closing: The end of a transaction process where the deed is delivered, documents are signed, and funds are dispersed.

CLUE (Comprehensive Loss Underwriting Exchange): The insurance industry's national database that assigns individuals a risk score. CLUE also has an electronic file of a properties insurance history. These files are accessible by insurance companies nationally. These files could impact the ability to sell property as they might contain information that a prospective buyer might find objectionable, and in some cases not even insurable.

Commission: The compensation paid to the listing brokerage by the seller for selling the property. A buyer may also be required to pay a commission to his or her agent.

Commission split: The percentage split of commission compensation between the real estate sales brokerage and the real estate sales agent or broker.

Comparative market analysis: A study done by real estate sales agents and brokers using active, pending, and sold comparable properties to estimate a listing price for a property.

Competitive Market Analysis (CMA): The analysis used to provide market information to the seller and assist the real estate broker in securing the listing.

Condominium association: An association of all owners in a condominium.

Condominium budget: A financial forecast and report of a condominium association's expenses and savings.

Condominium by-laws: Rules passed by the condominium association used in administration of the condominium property.

Condominium declarations: A document that legally establishes a condominium.

Condominium right of first refusal: A person or an association that has the first opportunity to purchase condominium real estate when it becomes available or the right to meet any other offer.

Condominium rules and regulation: Rules of a condominium association by which owners agree to abide.

Contingency: A provision in a contract requiring certain acts to be completed before the contract is binding.

Continue to show: When a property is under contract with contingencies, but the seller requests that the property continue to be shown to prospective buyers until contingencies are released.

Contract for deed: A sales contract in which the buyer takes possession of the property but the seller holds title until the loan is paid. Also known as an installment sale contract.

Contract of sale: An agreement between the third-party relocation company and the seller (transferee) whereby the third-party company purchases property owned by the seller.

Conventional mortgage: A type of mortgage that has certain limitations placed on it to meet secondary market guidelines. Mortgage companies, banks, and savings and loans underwrite conventional mortgages.

Cooperating commission: A commission offered to the buyer's agent brokerage for bringing a buyer to the selling brokerage's listing.

Cooperative (Co-op): Where the shareholders of the corporation are the inhabitants of the building. Each shareholder has the right to lease a specific unit. The difference between a co-op and a condo is in a co-op, one owns shares in a corporation; in a condo one owns the unit fee simple.

Corporate client: The company with whom the third-party relocation company has an agreement to handle the relocating employees.

Counteroffer: The response to an offer or a bid by the seller or buyer after the original offer or bid.

Credit report: Includes all of the history for a borrower's credit accounts, outstanding debts, and payment timelines on past or current debts.

Credit score: A score assigned to a borrower's credit report based on information contained therein.

Curb appeal: The visual impact a property projects from the street.

Days on market: The number of days a property has been on the market.

Decree: A judgment of the court that sets out the agreements and rights of the parties.

Desk fees: A fee charged by the real estate company or brokerage for the real estate agent to use a desk.

Destination services: Services provided to the transferee at the new location. They can include familiarization tours, temporary housing, school searches, and so on.

Direct home-selling costs (DHSC): Carrying costs, loss on sale, repairs and improvements, commission, closing costs, principal, interest, taxes and insurance, interest on equity loans, and utilities.

Disclosures: Federal, state, county, and local requirements of disclosure that the seller provides and the buyer acknowledges.

Divorce: The legal separation of a husband and wife effected by a court decree that totally dissolves the marriage relationship.

DOM: Days on market.

Down payment: The amount of cash put toward a purchase by the borrower.

Drive-by: When a buyer or seller agent or broker drives by a property listing or potential listing.

Dual agent: A state-licensed individual who represents the seller and the buyer in a single transaction.

Earnest money deposit: The money given to the seller at the time the offer is made as a sign of the buyer's good faith.

E-mail: Electronic or Internet-based communication.

Escrow account for real estate taxes and insurance: An account into which borrowers pay monthly prorations for real estate taxes and property insurance.

Exchange/service account: A brokerage expense account that accrues charges for marketing.

Exclusions: Fixtures or personal property that are excluded from the contract or offer to purchase.

Expired (listing): A property listing that has expired per the terms of the listing agreement.

Fax rider: A document that treats facsimile transmission as the same legal effect as the original document.

Feedback: The real estate sales agent and/or his or her client's reaction to a listing or property. Requested by the listing agent.

Fee simple: A form of property ownership where the owner has the right to use and dispose of property at will.

FHA: Federal Housing Administration.

FHA (Federal Housing Administration) Loan Guarantee: A guarantee by the FHA that a percentage of a loan will be underwritten by a mortgage company or banker.

Fixture: Personal property that has become part of the property through permanent attachment.

Flat fee: A predetermined amount of compensation received or paid for a specific service in a real estate transaction.

Floor duty or time: That a time, usually assigned, when a real estate sales agent answers telephones, e-mails, or walk-in requests for information on property.

For sale by owner (FSBO): A property that is for sale by the owner of the property.

Gift letter: A letter to a lender stating that a gift of cash has been made to the buyer(s) and that the person gifting the cash to the buyer is not expecting the gift to be repaid. The exact wording of the gift letter should be requested of the lender.

Good faith estimate: Under the Real Estate Settlement Procedures Act, within three days of an application submission, lenders are required to provide in writing to potential borrowers a good faith estimate of closing costs.

Gross closed commission income: The total amount of commission income a real estate sales agent or broker receives from closed transactions.

Gross sale price: The sale price before any concessions.

Guaranteed offer: The amount, after appraisals, the employer offers the transferring employee for his or her property.

Hazard insurance: Insurance that covers losses to real estate from damages that might affect its value.

Home-finding assistance: Additional assistance provided by a third-party relocation company that can include information about the destination community.

Homeowner's insurance: Coverage that includes personal liability and theft insurance in addition to hazard insurance.

HUD: Department of Housing and Urban Development.

HUD/RESPA (Housing and Urban Development/Real Estate Settlement Procedures Act): A document and statement that details all of the monies paid out and received at a real estate property closing.

Hybrid adjustable rate: Offers a fixed rate the first 5 years and then adjusts annually for the next 25 years.

IDX (Internet Data Exchange): Allows real estate brokers to advertise each other's listings posted to listing databases such as the multiple listing service.

Inclusions: Fixtures or personal property that are included in a contract or offer to purchase.

Independent contractor: A real estate sales agent who conducts real estate business through a broker. This agent does not receive salary or benefits from the broker.

Inputting: The process of entering new listings or changes to a current listing in the multiple listing services.

Inspection rider: Rider to purchase agreement between third party relocation company and buyer of transferee's property stating that property is being sold "as is." All inspection reports conducted by the third party company are disclosed to the buyer and it is the buyer's duty to do his/her own inspections and tests.

Installment land contract: A contract in which the buyer takes possession of the property while the seller retains the title to the property until the loan is paid.

Interest rate float: The borrower decides to delay locking their interest rate on their loan. They can float their rate in expectation of the rate moving down. At the end of the float period they must lock a rate.

Interest rate lock: When the borrower and lender agree to lock a rate on loan. Can have terms and conditions attached to the lock.

Inventory: A transferee's property the third party relocation company has acquired.

List date: Actual date the property was listed with the current broker.

List price: The price of a property through a listing agreement.

Listing: Brokers written agreement to represent a seller and their property. Agents refer to their inventory of agreements with sellers as listings.

Listing agent: The real estate sales agent that is representing the sellers and their property, through a listing agreement.

Listing agreement: A document that establishes the real estate agent's agreement with the sellers to represent their property in the market.

Listing appointment: The time when a real estate sales agent meets with potential clients selling a property to secure a listing agreement.

Listing exclusion: A clause included in the listing agreement when the seller (transferee) lists his or her property with a broker.

Loan: An amount of money that is lent to a borrower who agrees to repay the amount plus interest.

Loan application: A document that buyers who are requesting a loan fill out and submit to their lender.

Loan closing costs: The costs a lender charges to close a borrower's loan. These costs vary from lender to lender and from market to market.

Loan commitment: A written document telling the borrowers that the mortgage company has agreed to lend them a specific amount of money at a specific interest rate for a specific period of time.

The loan commitment may also contain conditions upon which the loan commitment is based.

Loan package: The group of mortgage documents that the borrower's lender sends to the closing or escrow.

Loan processor: An administrative individual who is assigned to check, verify, and assemble all of the documents and the buyer's funds and the borrower's loan for closing.

Loan underwriter: One who underwrites a loan for another. Some lenders have investors underwrite a buyer's loan.

Lockbox: A tool that allows secure storage of property keys on the premises for agent use. A combo uses a rotating dial to gain access with a combination; a Supra® (electronic lockbox or ELB) features a keypad.

Managing broker: A person licensed by the state as a broker who is also the broker of record for a real estate sales office. This person manages the daily operations of a real estate sales office.

Market familiarization trip: A visit by the transferee to the new location to view housing market options and location highlights.

Marketing period: The period of time in which the transferee may market his or her property (typically 45, 60, or 90 days), as directed by the third-party company's contract with the employer.

Mortgage banker: One who lends the bank's funds to borrowers and brings lenders and borrowers together.

Mortgage broker: A business that or an individual who unites lenders and borrowers and processes mortgage applications.

Mortgage loan servicing company: A company that collects monthly mortgage payments from borrowers.

Multiple listing service (MLS): A service that compiles available properties for sale by member brokers.

Multiple offers: More than one buyers broker present an offer on one property where the offers are negotiated at the same time.

National Association of REALTORS® (NAR): A national association comprised of real estate sales agents.

Net sales price: Gross sales price less concessions to the buyers.

Niche: A special area or interest.

Off market: A property listing that has been removed from the sale inventory in a market. A property can be temporarily or permanently off market.

Offer to purchase: When a buyer proposes certain terms and presents these terms to the seller.

Office tour/caravan: A walking or driving tour by a real estate sales office of listings represented by agents in the office. Usually held on a set day and time.

Open house (public): When a listing that is on market is available to the public for viewings and showings.

Parcel identification number (PIN): A taxing authority's tracking number for a property.

Payoff letter: A written document from a seller's mortgage company stating the amount of money needed to pay the loan in full.

Pending: A real estate contract that has been accepted on a property but the transaction has not closed.

Personal assistant: A real estate sales agent administrative assistant.

Planned unit development (PUD): Mixed-use development that sets aside areas for residential use, commercial use, and public areas such as schools, parks, and so on.

Preapproval: A higher level of buyer/borrower prequalification required by a mortgage lender. Some preapprovals have conditions the borrower must meet.

Prepaid interest: Funds paid by the borrower at closing based on the number of days left in the month of closing.

Prepayment penalty: A fine imposed on the borrower by the lender when the loan is paid off before it comes due.

Prequalification: The mortgage company tells a buyer in advance of the formal mortgage application, how much money the borrower can afford to borrow. Some prequalifications have conditions that the borrower must meet.

Preview appointment: When a buyer's agent views a property alone to see if it meets his or her buyer's needs.

Pricing: When the potential seller's agent goes to the potential listing property to view it for marketing and pricing purposes.

Principal: The amount of money a buyer borrows.

Principal, interest, taxes, and insurance (PITI): The four parts that make up a borrower's monthly mortgage payment.

Private mortgage insurance (PMI): A special insurance paid by a borrower in monthly installments, typically of loans of more than 80 percent of the value of the property.

Professional designation: Additional nonlicensed real estate education completed by a real estate professional.

Professional regulation: A state licensing authority that oversees and disciplines licensees.

Promissory note: A promise-to-pay document used with a contract or an offer to purchase.

Property or home-finding assistance status reports: Reports filed weekly or monthly by the listing or buying agent representing the transferee.

R & I: Estimated and actual repair and improvement costs.

Real estate agent: An individual who is licensed by the state and who acts on behalf of his or her client, the buyer or seller. The real estate agent who does not have a broker's license must work for a licensed broker.

Real estate contract: A binding agreement between buyer and seller. It consists of an offer and an acceptance as well as consideration (i.e., money).

REALTOR®: A registered trademark of the National Association of REALTORS® that can be used only by its members.

Release deed: A written document stating that a seller or buyer has satisfied his or her obligation on a debt. This document is usually recorded.

Relist: Property that was listed with another broker but relisted with a current broker.

Rider: A separate document that is attached to a document in some way. This is done so that an entire document does not need to be rewritten.

Salaried agent: A real estate sales agent or broker who receives all or part of his or her compensation in real estate sales in the form of a salary.

Sale price: The price paid for a listing or property.

Sales meetings: An informational meeting conducted by the managing broker held in the real estate sales office.

Sales volume: The total amount of all sales prices for all transactions completed by a real estate agent, broker, or real estate sales office.

Secondary market: An institutional investment market that purchases mortgages from mortgage lenders.

Seller (owner): The owner of a property who has signed a listing agreement or a potential listing agreement.

Showing: When a listing is shown to prospective buyers or the buyer's agent (preview).

Sign rider: An additional sign placed on a brokerage yard sign; it may include the agent's name, "open Sunday," "contract pending," "sold," the new price, and so on.

Special assessment: A special and additional charge to a unit in a condominium or cooperative. Also a special real estate tax for improvements that benefit a property.

State Association of REALTORS®: An association of REALTORS® in a specific state.

Supra®: An electronic lockbox (ELB) that holds keys to a property. The user must have a Supra keypad to use the lockbox.

Temporarily off market (TOM): A listed property that is taken off the market due to illness, travel, needed repairs, and so on.

Temporary housing: Housing a transferee occupies until permanent housing is selected or becomes available.

Third-party company: A relocation company hired by an employee's employer to coordinate the employee's move to a new location.

Trailing spouse: The spouse or partner of the employee being moved to a new location by an employer.

Transaction: The real estate process from offer to closing or escrow.

Transaction fee: A fixed amount in addition to commission charged to sellers.

Transaction management fee (TMF): A fee charged by listing brokers to the seller as part of the listing agreement.

Transaction sides: The two sides of a transaction, sellers and buyers. The term used to record the number of transactions in which a real estate sales agent or broker was involved during a specific period.

24-hour notice: Allowed by law, tenants must be informed of showing 24 hours before you arrive.

Under contract: A property that has an accepted real estate contract between seller and buyer.

VA: Veterans Administration

VA (Veterans Administration) Loan Guarantee: A guarantee on a mortgage amount backed by the Department of Veterans Affairs.

Vacate date: The date on which the seller (transferee) vacates the property (generally the date when responsibility for property expense by the transferee ends) and the third-party company assumes ownership for the property through a buyout.

Virtual tour: An Internet web/CD-ROM-based video presentation of a property.

Voice mail: A telephone message system where voice messages can be retrieved directly or from a remote location.

VOW's (Virtual Office web sites): An Internet based real estate brokerage business model that works with real estate consumers in same way as a brick and mortar real estate brokerage.

W-2: The Internal Revenue form issued by employer to employee to reflect compensation and deductions to compensation.

W-9: The Internal Revenue form requesting taxpayer identification number and certification.

Walk-through: A showing before closing or escrow that permits the buyers one final tour of the property they are purchasing.

Will: A document by which a person disposes of his or her property after death.

Work sheet (transaction): The real estate sales company form that records all information relevant to a transaction.

Housing Types

Condominium/Cooperative/Apartment Terms

Common area/grounds: The elements of building and grounds that all unit owners own jointly.

Condominium: A dwelling of two or more property units where the owner owns the interior space and, in common with other owners, owns a square foot ratio of the common areas, such as the grounds, hallways, stairways, lobby, mechanical systems of common areas, and parking and recreational areas.

Cooperative (Co-op): A corporation in which the tenants purchase shares that give them the right to occupy a unit in the building.

Courtyard: An outdoor space faced by a building.

Duplex: Two properties joined by one common wall.

Elevator building: One that has one or more elevators to reach the units.

Flat: Another name for an apartment.

Full-amenity building: One that offers a variety of services to occupants: doorman, delivery/shipping room, dry cleaner, pool, tennis court, store, exercise facilities, and so on.

Garden apartment: A dwelling unit partially below grade.

High-rise: A multiple-floor building of ten or more floors.

Management company: A professional real estate management company that manages the physical operation of a building.

On-site management: The management of a building who works from an office within the building.

Parking:
- Deeded: A parking space that is owned as a piece of real estate.
- Leased: A parking space that is leased by the building occupant.
- Underground: A parking space located beneath grade of the building.
- Assigned: A parking space appointed by the association or management company.
- Valet: The car is parked and returned by a parking attendant for the occupant of the space.

Self-managed: Buildings and dwelling units overseen by unit owners or unit shareholders.

Site engineer: The mechanical or operations professional for a building who is on-site at his or her place of employment. Some engineers live on the premises and are referred to as the super, short for superintendent.

Walk-up: A building with no elevator.

Other Property Terms

Income/investment property: Property that provides compensation or tax advantages to the owner.

1-4 unit: A multiple-dwelling building of one to four units.

2/3 flat: A multiple-dwelling building that has two or three units stacked on top of each other.

Lakefront: A dwelling unit that has front footage on a lake.

Lake view: A dwelling unit that has visual exposure to a lake.

Manufactured home: All or part of a dwelling unit that is constructed in one location and placed in another location.

Mid-rise: A multiple-floor building that has three to nine floors.

Mobile home: A dwelling unit that is constructed with attached wheels and can be moved from one location to another.

Model home/condo: A dwelling unit that the builder/developer finishes as a sales sample for the public to view.

Penthouse: A dwelling unit of the uppermost occupied floor of a building.

Percent owner-occupied: The number of units in a condo or co-op that are owner-occupied.

Rental: Property for which the occupant/tenant pays the landlord/owner a fixed periodical sum of money.

Riparian: Property rights relating to land bordering flowing water.

Row houses: Attached homes with a common side wall(s).

Quadrominium: Four attached condominiums.

Single-family home: A dwelling unit that has no common walls with another dwelling unit.

Spec home: A home built on speculation by a builder/developer.

Studio: A one-room dwelling unit.

Town house: A series of attached dwelling units with common wall(s).

Vacation or resort or second home: A residence owned as a nonprimary residence.

Water rights: Rights by a property owner to use a body of water.

House styles:
American Four Square
Bi-level
Brownstone
Bungalow
Cape Cod
Coach House
Colonial
- Dutch
- Center Entry
- Federal
- Georgian
- Williamsburg

Contemporary
Cottage
Earth Home
English Basement
Farmhouse
French Provincial
Georgian
Greystone
Hillside
Landmark
Log
Mediterranean
Prairie
Queen Anne

Rambler
Ranch
Raised Ranch
Row House
Spanish
Split Level
Traditional
Tri-level
Tudor-English
Victorian
Walk-out (basement)

New construction terms:

Allowance
Option
Package
Proposed
Stubbed bath
Upgrade

Property feature terms:

Air conditioning
Central air
Space pac
Window/wall
Zoned

Basement/Foundation:

Block: Concrete
Brick
Cellar: A room for storing garden products, i.e., bulbs, canned goods, and so on
Concrete
Crawl space: A shallow space beneath the first floor
English: One that is partially above grade
Exterior access: One that has a door to the outside

Finished: One that has drywalled or paneled rooms

Full: One that is the same size as the first floor, excluding the garage

Partial: One that does not cover the same area as the first floor

Partially finished: One that has drywall or paneled walls

Piers/pillars: Supports under a dwelling unit

Slab: A concrete slab foundation

Stone: Stone as side walls of foundation

Unfinished: One that has no finished space

Walk-out: One that has a door to the outside

Wood: One that has side walls or the floor constructed from wood

Baths:

Master

Full

Powder

Bidet

Driveway:

Shared

Electrical:

Circuit breakers

Fuses

Amps

Safety Equipment:

CO Detectors

Smoke/Fire Detectors

Exterior Materials:

Aluminum

Asbestos

Block

Brick

Cedar
Dryvit
Frame
Glass
Log
Marble/Granite
Masonite
Shakes
Slate
Steel
Stone
Stucco
Vinyl

Fireplaces:
Decorative
Electric
Gas logs
Gas starter
Heatilator
Wood-burning

Flooring Types:
Carpet
Ceramic tile
Concrete
Hardwood
- Pegged
- Parquet
- Random-width

Marble
Vinyl

Garages:
Attached
Carport

Detached
Garage door openers
Transmitters

Heat/Fuel:
Baseboard
Electric
Gas
Gravity air
Forced air
Heat pump
Hot water/steam
Oil
Propane
Radiant
Radiators
Solar

Laundry:
First-floor laundry
In-unit laundry
Second-floor laundry

Miscellaneous Rooms:
Darkroom
Den/office/study
Exercise room
Foyer
Gallery
Great room
In-law arrangement
Lanai
Library
Loft
Maid's room
Porch, enclosed

Porch, screened
Recreation room
Sitting room
Workshop

Roof Types:

Asphalt rolled
Asphalt shingles
Copper
Fiberglass rolled
Fiberglass shingles
Metal
Rubber
Slate
Tar and gravel
Tile
Tin
Wood shakes/shingles

Construction terms:

Cathedral ceiling
Dry bar
Handicapped accessible
Handicapped equipped
Portico
Skylight
Wet bar

Chapter 10

Building a Solid Foundation

The Future of Residential Real Estate Sales

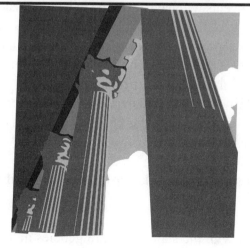

The graying of the real estate sales agent profession.

There is a growing demand and opportunity for new agents in real estate sales. Many trade publications discuss the average agent age (52 years) and the need to attract new and younger agents. How to attract these new agents seems to be the big question. This book, which explores the life of a real estate sales agent and provides information about this exciting and rewarding career, is one way to help bring people into the business. What can you do to improve your chances of succeeding at real estate sales? Be realistic about the business and the returns you can expect in Years 1, 2, and 3. You must be able to invest and reinvest in yourself. Those investments include personal commitments and training in marketing, time management, technology, and sales. You need to enter the real estate sales business with enough financial reserves to cover your expenses for six months to one year.

Real estate brokerage profit margins are slim. In the next couple of years, financial pressures will push brokerages to grow market share to maintain profit margins. Incremental costs for new technology and office expenses may be passed on to the real estate sales agent. Unproductive agents will have less time to increase sales volume before they are asked to reduce their commission split or leave the company. How can you ensure that you are successful early on? You must implement your annual business plan, be able to reinvest in your business, find creative markets to prospect to, and be able to communicate efficiently with clients. Take time to look into some of the resources listed in the back of this book to get an idea of how vast and evolving real estate sales are.

Homeowner's insurance takes forefront as possible contract contingency.

We're familiar with the standard contingencies in home purchase agreements, but you should know that the ability for homebuyers to secure homeowner's insurance on a property, as well as their ability to secure it at a reasonable cost, may be a growing issue for buyers and sellers.

CLUE (Comprehensive Loss Underwriting Exchange) is the insurance industry's national database that assigns individuals a risk score. CLUE also has an electronic file of a property's insurance history. These files are accessible by insurance companies nationally. These files can impact the salability of property if they contain information a prospective buyer finds objectionable and in some cases may result in the property being uninsurable.

What is the recipe for a client's CLUE file? First is his or her personal credit file data. On a yearly basis, a client should make sure his or her credit history is up to date and accurate. A poor credit rating can impact a person's ability to secure homeowner's insurance. After the credit history comes the house's claim history from the last five years. One should be cautious about calling an insurance agent about marginal losses; even zero-payout losses are recorded in the database.

Buyers should ask their real estate sales agent to write a homeowner's insurance contingency into the purchase offer to see if they can procure insurance and at what cost. Sellers need to get a copy of their CLUE report before placing their property for sale to see what, if any, surprises are in the report and whether they can be corrected or addressed with prospective buyers.

Virtual Office web sites (VOWs) and what they mean to the future of real estate.

VOWs allow real estate brokers to display all for-sale property listings within an MLS. The information is available to users who provide the VOW with information about themselves and their home purchase or sale parameters. Property data can be included even if the listing broker decides not to participate (opt-out) in the Internet Data Exchange. The Internet Data Exchange allows real estate brokers to display one another's listings on their own brokerage web sites, with one another's permission.

The future is here for the residential real estate industry via the World Wide Web. Many major players are not happy with the evolution of the Internet with regard to their business models. A majority of real estate consumers begin their home search or extract property information from the web sites of brokerages, newspapers, real estate associations, and multiple listing services.

Should real estate consumers be concerned with new proposals before real estate trade organizations that may impact their ability to find property information on the Internet? Yes. As traditional real estate brokerages have begun placing their listing information on the Internet, they are no longer the "keepers of information."

There is growing polarization between traditional brokerages and the newer VOWs over who can use opt in or-opt out listing information on the web sites. VOWs have increased their market share and are referring growing numbers of clients to real estate sales agents. I receive many e-mail advertisements from VOWs that generate leads for my real estate business. Usually, these leads come from real estate consumers visiting and logging into real estate web sites looking for properties. The shift in how leads are generated for brokerages is the basic issue for traditional brokerages. Traditional brokerages don't want their listing information, which they have worked hard to secure, to be used by VOWs to generate income streams from referral fees paid by real estate sales agents looking for client leads.

Stay tuned on this issue. It may be this Internet-based rift that starts to dramatically change the residential real estate business model that has been in place.

Virtual Tours: Go home shopping without leaving home!

After years of taking home buyers out to look at properties in the market, I learned that many buyers decide just inside the front door that the property doesn't work for them. In most instances, they tell me this fact, and sometimes their body language conveys the message! And this experience is after our discussions about their home needs and wants. Home buyers like to drive their own home purchase process. A new way for them to see a large number of available homes from the comfort of their home or office is to view virtual tours of homes for sale in the geographical area in which they are interested.

What is a virtual tour? A virtual tour is a digitized or electronic file of one or more exterior or interior images of a property. Typically, the camera pans 360 degrees to capture the entire perspective from where the camera is placed. Virtual tours provide a good overall feeling of the location, but smaller rooms or spaces can be distorted. Also, windows with strong natural light coming in can be seen as white space. Virtual tours are a great way for buyers and their agents to preview a property before deciding whether to visit it in person.

Most sellers, once their property can be viewed via a virtual tour, understand the marketing power of the Internet and prospective home buyers' ability to shop "off-site" for a home. When no virtual tour is available, some sellers' properties can be missed by the growing numbers of buyers who conduct their entire home search on the Internet. A couple of years ago I had an upper-bracket listing. The buyer, who had just accepted a position in Chicago, was house hunting without his spouse, who was at their home in Europe. The buyer liked the listing but wanted to know if it would still be available in three weeks when his spouse came to join him. The real estate market at the time was moving fast, so I suggested to the buyer's agent that the gentleman's spouse go to my brokerage web site and take the virtual tour. The spouse took the tour from her home in Europe and called the buyer spouse in Chicago and gave the green light to purchase the home!

In some situations, security issues for home sellers can put the lens cap on a virtual tour of their property. Privacy issues can also make some sellers uneasy. Government rulings protect one's privacy at home, but homeowners should be aware that once a virtual of tour of their home is on the Web, they give up all reasonable expectations of privacy.

As technology advances in virtual tours, look for better image quality and larger numbers of images. Sellers should remember the 24/7 rule of the Internet: No one wants a buyer in his or her home for a showing at 11 p.m., but at 11 p.m., from the comfort of his or her own home, a buyer can get a good idea of what is available and to his or her liking. Buyers begin their home search on the Internet. If they see a property they like that has only a still photo (and no virtual tour icon), they call the listing agent to see if a tour is available. If not, they suggest that the listing agent join the growing numbers of seller, buyers, and real estate sales agents who have discovered the power of the virtual tour.

Are the days numbered for real estate agents to cold-call using the telephone?

Annoying telemarketing calls by consumer product companies can come to an end when you register on the national "Do Not Call" list. But an early exemption was real estate and insurance agents. It appeared to be a victory for those agents who worked cross and telephone directories to dial someone's home and pitch their real estate or insurance services. But newer guidelines put the burden on the real estate or insurance agent to purchase and cross-check the "Do Not Call" lists before picking up the phone. Hefty fines await the agent who dials first and doesn't check to see if the number has been registered. Consumers have enthusiastically welcomed the "Do Not Call" registery to protect their privacy and time.

I am not an advocate of cold-calling in my real estate business. When I first started in real estate sales, many national motivational speakers pitched their telemarketing prospecting products to agents. My business was based on recent trends in consumer-product marketing that focused on building relationships with consumers first and selling my services second. It worked and did not involve a hard sell — just reliable, professional real estate services on the consumer's timeline.

Is this the end of an era for real estate sales agent telemarketing? Perhaps, so families can get through dinner without being inter-rupted by pesky telemarketers, real estate sales agents included. Another change that the real estate industry needs to understand is that the consumer and their needs come first. If the industry can't address what consumers want, it must find or create another real estate business model that does address their needs.

The Internet and its impact on real estate sales.

More buyers and sellers use the Internet before contacting a real estate sales agent. Check media sources for statistics on Internet consumer habits. On-line mortgage applications, Internet web site-based transaction management, and search engines growing their real estate presence can impact how the Internet consumer does or doesn't get to you. Gather information in your market on Internet-based brokerages and the differences between them and your company. Many people in the real estate sales business have not perceived these new virtual brokerages as a threat. On-line brokerages will continue to erode market share for traditional brokerage businesses; virtual brokerages are reaching consumers early on in their property searches and building relationships with them.

Compensation for service and salaried agents come of age.

The Internet-educated real estate consumer will demand new compensation models for transaction service providers. The new consumer compensation models will impact how brokerages compensate their real estate sales agents. One compensation model that has been tested successfully in some markets is a salaried agent. Monitor what mainstream media and real estate trade organizations are reporting on these emerging compensation issues.

Banks as real estate brokerages.

Additional competitive pressure is coming from banks and financial holding companies that would like to offer real estate brokerage services to their customers. The real estate brokerage industry is fighting to keep this potential new competitor at bay. Both groups have strong lobbying and financial backing to fight the battle. Watch for developments on this issue. The ability of banks and financial institutions to offer real estate brokerage services will have a definite impact on the real estate sales business.

Add "mold" to your property inspection lists.

In 2001, the issue of mold arrived at the forefront of real estate business. Sales agents must realize the impact it can have on the sale of properties they represent. This new inspection buzzword may be heard throughout the transaction. Talk to your managing broker or mentor about the effects of mold in your market. Below are some tips from the U.S. Consumer Product Safety Commission that consumers can use when shopping for a home:

- Look for rotted building materials. They suggest moisture or water damage.
- Look for obvious mold growth in attics, basements, and crawl

spaces and around the foundation.
- Make sure downspouts from roof gutters route water away from the building.
- Look for plants close to the house, particularly if they are damp and rotting. They are a source of biological pollutants.
- Look for moisture on windows and surfaces.
- Look for signs of leaks or seepage in the basement.
- Look for stains on walls, floors, and carpets, including carpet over concrete floors.
- Check that the kitchen cooktop has a hood vented outside.
- Check that the clothes dryer is vented outside.
- Check for exhaust fans in the bathrooms.
- Make sure all vents lead outdoors and not into attics or crawl spaces.
- Check that ventless rooms have at least one window that opens to the outside.
- Hire a professional to check the heating and cooling system, including a humidifier and vents. Have him or her check duct lining and insulation for mold growth.

The only constant is change.

The next year in real estate sales will be an exciting one for all involved as consumerism grows within the industry. How this consumerism manifests itself and the reaction from the industry will impact how the real estate sales business model evolves. This exciting time allows the industry to be creative and position itself for the new age of real estate sales consumerism. Remain up to date on changing consumer trends, be innovative, listen to clients, add value to transactions, have a plan, and work it!

A

Accredited Buyer Representative ABR
www.rebac.net

Alabama Association of REALTORS®
www.alabamarealtors.com

Alaska Association of REALTORS®
http://realtorsofalaska.com

American Society of Farm Managers and Rural Appraisers
www.asfmra.org

American Society of Home Inspectors
www.ashi.com

AOL Home Price Check
www.aol.homepricecheck.com

The Appraisal Foundation
www.appraisalfoundation.org

Appraisal Institute
www.appraisalinstitute.org

Arizona Association of REALTORS®
www.aaronline.com

Arkansas REALTORS®Association
www.arkansasrealtors.com

C

California Association of REALTORS®
www.car.org

The Canadian Real Estate Association
www.crea.ca

Century 21
www.century21.com

Council of Residential Specialists
www.crs.com

Certified International Property Specialists Network
www.cipsnetwork.com

Citimortgage
www.iown.com

Coldwell Banker
www.coldwellbanker.com

Colorado Association of REALTORS®
www.colorealtor.org

Crossroads Relocation (National Gay and Lesbian)
www.crossroadsrelocation.org

D

Dearborn Real Estate Education
www.dearborn.com

Dearborn Trade Publishing
www.dearborntrade.com

Delaware Association of REALTORS®
www.delawarerealtor.com

Department of Veterans Affairs
www.va.gov

E

The Educated Home Buyer
www.educatedhomebuyer.com

Employee Relocation Council
www.erc.org

e-PRO
www.epronar.com

ERA.com
www.era.com

EverythingRE.com
www.everythingre.com

F

Fannie Mae
www.fanniemae.com

Florida Association of REALTORS®
http://planetrealtor.com

Florida Manufactured Homes Magazine
www.mcxpress.com

Freddie Mac
www.freddiemac.com

G

Georgia Association of REALTORS®
www.garealtor.com

GMAC RE
www.gmacre.com

Graduate Realtor® Institute
www.edesignations.com

H

Hawaii Association of REALTORS®
www.hawaiirealtors.com

Homes.com
www.homes.com

Homestead
www.homestead.com

House Values .com
www.housevalues.com

HUD
www.hud.org

I

Idaho Association of REALTORS®
www.idahorealtors.com

iHouse 2000
www.ihouse2000.com

Illinois Association of REALTORS®
www.illinoisrealtor.org

Illinois Office of Banks and Real Estate
www.obre.state.il.us/

Indiana Association of REALTORS®
www.indianarealtors.com

Inman News Features
www.inman.com

Institute of Real Estate Management
www.irem.org

International Real Estate Digest
www.ired.com

K

Kansas Association of REALTORS®
www.kansasrealtor.com

Keller Williams Realty
www.kw.com

Kentucky Association of REALTORS®
www.kar.com

L

Land Journal
www.landjournal.com

Louisiana REALTORS®
www.larealtors.org

M

Magnet Street
www.magnetstreet.com

Maine Association of REALTORS®
www.mainerealtors.com

Manufactured Housing Institute
www.manufacturedhousing.org

MapQuest
www.mapquest.com

Maryland Association of REALTORS®
www.mdrealtor.org

Massachusetts Association of REALTORS®
www.marealtor.com

Michigan Association of REALTORS®
www.mirealtors.com

Minnesota Association of REALTORS®
www.mnrealtor.com

Modern Postcard
www.modernpostcard.com

monstermoving.com
www.virtualrelocation.com

Mortgage Bankers Association of America
www.mbaa.org

Mortgage Credit Problems.com
www.mortgagecreditproblems.com

MSN House & Home
http://houseandhome.msn.com

N

National Apartment Association
www.naahq.org

National Association of Home Builders
www.nahb.com

National Association of Mortgage Brokers
www.namb.org

National Association of Real Estate Appraisers
www.iami.org

National Association of Real Estate Brokers
www.nareb.com

National Association of Real Estate Editors
www.naree.org

National Association of REALTORS®
www.realtor.com
www.realtor.org

National Property Management Association
www.npma.org

The Real Estate Educators Association
www.reea.org

New Hampshire Association of REALTORS®
www.nhar.com

New Jersey Association of REALTORS®
www.njar.com

New York State Association of REALTORS®
www.nysar.com

North Carolina Association of REALTORS®
www.ncrealtors.org

North Dakota Association of REALTORS®
www.ndrealtors.com

O

Ohio Association of REALTORS®
www.ohiorealtors.org

Oklahoma Association of REALTORS®
www.oklahomarealtors.com

Online Realty Sales.com
www.onlinerealtysales.com

P

Post Card Press
www.postcardpress.com

PrivateForSale.com
www.privateforsale.com

Prudential Real Estate
www.prudentialrealestate.com

R

RealEstate Abc
www.realestateabc.com

RealEstateAgencies.net
www.realestateagencies.net

Real Estate Auction Guide
www.realestateauctionguide.com

Real Estate Clipart.com
www.realestateclipart.com

RealEstate.com
www.realestate.com

Real-Marketing.com
www.real-marketing.com

The Real Estate Library
www.relibrary.com

The Real Estate Professional Magazine
www.therealestatepro.com

REALTORS® Land Institute
www.rliland.com

Realty Times
http://realtytimes.com

Rebuz
http://rebuz.com

RE/MAX.com
www.remax.com

Rhode Island Association of REALTORS®
www.riliving.com

RISMedia
www.rismedia.com

S

Seniors Real Estate Specialist
www.seniorsrealestate.com

Society of Industrial and Office REALTORS®
www.sior.com

South Carolina Association of REALTORS®
www.screaltors.com

South Dakota Association of REALTORS®
www.sdrealtor.org

State of Connecticut Department of Banking
www.state.ct.us/dob

T

Tennessee Association of REALTORS®
www.tarnet.com

Texas Association of REALTORS®
www.texasrealtors.com

U

Utah Association of REALTORS®
www.utahrealtors.com

V

Vandema Commercial Real Estate Resources
www.vandema.com

Vermont Association of REALTORS®
www.vtrealtor.com

Virginia Association of REALTORS®
www.varealtor.com

W

Wisconsin REALTORS® Association
www.wra.org

Women's Council of REALTORS®
www.wcr.org

Index

About the Author

Mark Nash, author of *The Original New Agent's Guide: Starting & Succeeding in Real Estate*, has garnered five-star reviews from the Midwest Book Review and the National Association of REALTORS® as well as national media focus on Bloomberg TV. His second book, *The Financial Power of Niche Marketing* originally published in June of 2003. Mark founded the Training Institute, L.L.C., of Illinois, which provides state-approved prelicense real estate education, technology, and sales training in Illinois. In 2001, The TrainingInstituteOnline.com web site received the Golden Web Award for outstanding web content, site navigation, and design. In addition to his real estate education business, Mark markets residential real estate brokerage transaction services to the public through his affiliation with Koenig & Strey/ GMAC Real Estate, targeting real estate consumers through MarkNashRealtor.com, a 2001 Golden Web Award winner for site content and navigation. Mark has been a Presidents Club member since 1999. Previous to Koenig & Strey/GMAC, he was affiliated with Prudential Preferred Properties, where he was involved in creating their "Prestige Homes" marketing program for niche upper-bracket properties. Mark is a member of Presidents Circle, which is comprised of the top 5 percent of sales associates with Prudential Real Estate nationally. In his first five years in real estate, he went from a novice to the annual top-tier producer in residential real estate sales.

Mark's consistent growth in real estate sales was acquired through implementation of niche and segment marketing in his consumer product sales experience representing international brands—Bristol Meyers, Clairol, and Duracell. He utilizes the success of target and niche marketing campaigns from his consumer product sales history to appeal to niches and subgroups in real estate sales. Mark was involved in field training sales representatives with consumer product companies in Indiana, Illinois, Michigan, and Wisconsin. He received consumer product sales leader awards multiple years in the 1990s. Mark's interest in real estate began in the 1980s as he became a successful nonlicensed investor in new construction and income properties. He studied in Athens, Greece, in the mid '70s as part of a University of Wisconsin program. His appreciation of architecture and cultural and ethnic diversity was established during his studies in Europe.

Visit Mr. Nash's other real estate-related web site:
• www.realtynewsonline.org